# Focus on Toddlers:

## How-tos and What-to-dos when Caring for Toddlers and Twos

Also by Jennifer Karnopp:

*Family Child Care Basics: Advice, Activities, and Information to Create a Professional Program*

*Elementos de un Cuidado de Niños Hogareño: Consejos, Actividades e Información para Crear un Programa Profesional*

*Focus on Babies: How-tos and What-to-dos when Caring for Infants*

GH10511
A Gryphon House Book

# FOCUS ON

## How-tos and What-to-dos when Caring for Toddlers and Twos

# TODDLERS

Jennifer Karnopp

Illustrations by Deb Johnson

**Gryphon House, Inc.**
Lewisville, NC

Cover photograph courtesy of iStockphoto.
Illustrations by Deb Johnson.
Photographs courtesy of iStockphoto.

Library of Congress Cataloging-in-Publication Data

Karnopp, Jennifer.
  Focus on toddlers : how-tos and what-to-dos when caring for toddlers and twos / by Jennifer Karnopp ; illustrations by Deb Johnson.
       p. cm.
  Includes index.
  ISBN 978-0-87659-380-6
  1. Child care. 2. Toddlers--Care. 3. Early childhood education. 4. Child care services. I. Title.
  HQ778.5.K374 2012
  649'.1--dc23
                        2012004429

Bulk Purchase
Gryphon House books are available for special premiums and sales promotions as well as for fund-raising use. Special editions or book excerpts also can be created to specifications. For details, contact the Director of Marketing at Gryphon House.

Disclaimer
Gryphon House, Inc. cannot be held responsible for damage, mishap, or injury incurred during the use of or because of activities in this book. Appropriate and reasonable caution and adult supervision of children involved in activities and corresponding to the age and capability of each child involved is recommended at all times. Do not leave children unattended at any time. Observe safety and caution at all times.

# Contents

# Introduction

## Purpose

A quality learning environment is important for the healthy development of young children. The toddler years are unique, and what works for preschool does not always work with toddlers. In this book, you will find information and ideas to help you create a quality early learning program specifically for the toddlers in your care. While safety is always an important concern of any program, safety issues, rules, and regulations are not the focus of this book. Instead, we will take a look at the many elements that make up a quality early learning program. We will explore ideas for your physical space, your daily routines, your relationships and interactions with children and their families, and the experiences you create. After reading this book, you will be able to create a center-based program perfectly suited to meet the unique needs of toddlers and their families and suited to you, the caregiver, as well.

## Developmentally Appropriate Practice

As an early learning professional, you may feel pressured to "teach" toddlers or focus on their cognitive development. You want the children in your care to learn, and so it may be tempting to use materials designed for preschoolers and just water the activities down. But toddlers are not young preschoolers, and treating them as such is not developmentally appropriate. Their bodies and brains are developing rapidly. They need to spend their days learning to coordinate their bodies; to experiment with sounds, people, and objects; and to explore the world around them. This takes all of their energy and focus. As they do this, they are constantly making new discoveries and problem solving. To help toddlers grow and develop at their own pace, we need to encourage their independent explorations.

When we create a developmentally appropriate environment, we give children opportunities to practice and perfect discoveries that they have already made (the skills they have at their

current level of development) and then encourage them to problem solve and try new things (to push themselves toward the next level of development). In other words, developmentally appropriate practice is the art of encouraging children to perfect old skills and to explore new ones without getting bored or frustrated.

To help you create a developmentally appropriate toddler program, we will first explore the role of the caregiver. We will examine the elements of a good environment and how to plan and evaluate your program and routine, and we will give you information on toddler growth and development. You will also find some basic information on working with children with special needs.

A young child develops and grows as a whole child, meaning that all areas of development are interconnected. As a toddler learns to manipulate objects, such as removing a toy from a shelf, she is developing motor skills. When she hears us name the object that she grabs, she is developing language skills. When she smiles at us as she carries the toy to us and we react with a smile, we are encouraging social skills and emotional development. The child then takes in all of these experiences and information to develop a better understanding of the object and of her own abilities. *The toy is heavy, but I am able to carry it. It is safe to grab and carry. There is a word that describes the toy. When I carry the toy, my caregiver smiles at me. I feel good inside.* Improved abilities in one area of development enable a child to further explore another area. And when a child can better explore the world, she can better understand the world. For this reason, the rest of this book is devoted to activities that will help you meet the needs of the toddlers in your care in all areas of their development. Here the words *activity* and *experience* are used interchangeably to mean a planned, open-ended experience. We have divided our activities into four sections.

- **Social and Emotional:** experiences that encourage social interactions and bonding and promote healthy emotional development
- **Language:** experiences that promote early language development and communication skills
- **Motor:** experiences that develop both fine and gross motor skills
- **Sensory:** experiences that encourage sensory (touch, taste, smell, sound, sight) awareness

Each activity also includes a "tips" section in which you will find ideas for natural, playful ways to incorporate cognitive development, as well as other developmental areas, into each activity. We have not included a separate activity section for cognitive development because a toddler's cognitive development depends on the development of each of the above areas. When a toddler piles blocks into a tower, she is using motor skills; when she knocks the tower down and hears and feels the crash, she is promoting her own sensory development. When these experiences are looked at together, she is exploring cause and effect. That understanding is a cognitive skill. Instead of a dedicated cognitive section, you will discover that the exploratory nature of each activity gives toddlers all kinds of opportunities to develop age-appropriate thinking skills.

## A Guide to the Activities

The activities or experiences in this book are divided into four different developmental areas. Each activity's developmental area is marked in the upper right-hand corner of the page, and each has a corresponding icon. The upper right-hand corner also lets you know the appropriate ages for the activity, where it will work best, and how long to expect to prepare for it. Keep in mind, the ages are just approximations, so do not feel bound by them. All children are different. You know the toddlers you are working with. However, take care not to push a child to do an activity that she is not interested in, as that is probably a sign that she is not ready for it.

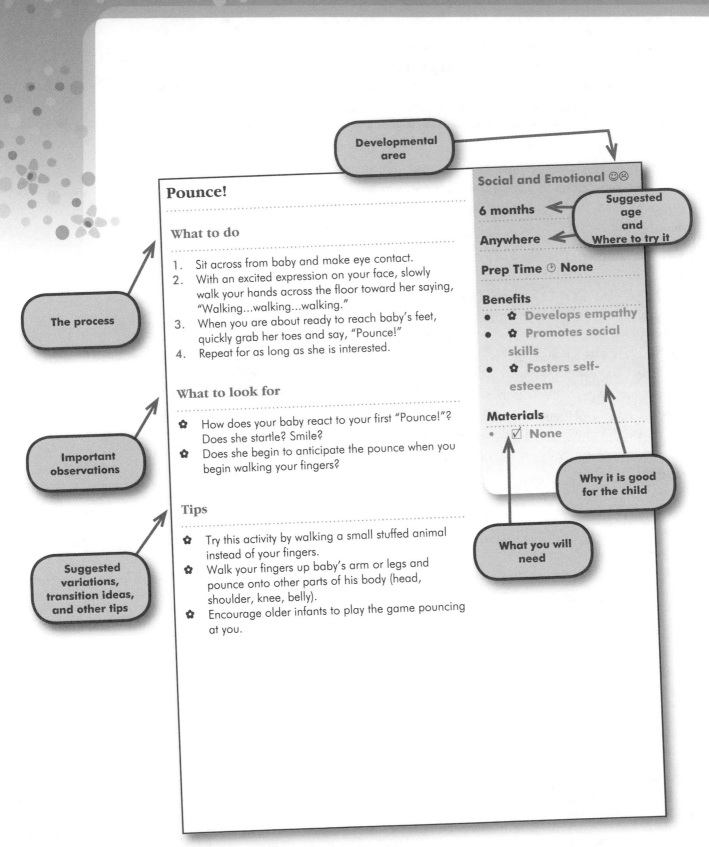

**Developmental area**

**The process**

**Important observations**

**Suggested variations, transition ideas, and other tips**

## Pounce!

### What to do

1. Sit across from baby and make eye contact.
2. With an excited expression on your face, slowly walk your hands across the floor toward her saying, "Walking...walking...walking."
3. When you are about ready to reach baby's feet, quickly grab her toes and say, "Pounce!"
4. Repeat for as long as she is interested.

### What to look for

✿ How does your baby react to your first "Pounce!"? Does she startle? Smile?
✿ Does she begin to anticipate the pounce when you begin walking your fingers?

### Tips

✿ Try this activity by walking a small stuffed animal instead of your fingers.
✿ Walk your fingers up baby's arm or legs and pounce onto other parts of his body (head, shoulder, knee, belly).
✿ Encourage older infants to play the game pouncing at you.

**Social and Emotional** ☺☹

**6 months**

**Anywhere**

**Suggested age and Where to try it**

**Prep Time** 🕐 **None**

**Benefits**
● ✿ Develops empathy
● ✿ Promotes social skills
● ✿ Fosters self-esteem

**Materials**
● ☑ None

**Why it is good for the child**

**What you will need**

# Chapter 1:
# The Role of the Caregiver

A toddler room is very different from a preschool classroom. The furniture is different, the routine is different, and the activities are different. So it makes sense that the role of the caregiver, or teacher, is also very different. When working with very young children, the caregiver needs to be a good child observer. Toddlers are always busy exploring their environments and learning about all of the things their bodies can do. They naturally turn every experience into a learning experience. As a caregiver, your role is to get to know each of the toddlers in your care and to create a warm, safe environment to encourage their explorations.

## Developing Attachment

An important developmental step for both infants and toddlers is to feel emotionally attached to the adult who is caring for them. This feeling of attachment helps them to develop trust and gives them a strong emotional foundation on which they can build many other skills. Most children naturally develop attachment to their family members, and this bond is extremely important. However, a toddler can feel attached to more than one person and should also feel attached to his caregiver. After all, you are the person responding to his needs while his family members are away. All caregivers should set the important goal of promoting this feeling of attachment in their child care settings.

Group size and the caregiver-to-child ratio are crucial for encouraging effective bonding. If the group is too large, or if children are cared for by too many different people, toddlers will not be responded to consistently and sensitively. Each state has its own guidelines for licensing, but if you would like more guidance, consider following these recommended minimum caregiver-to-child-ratio guidelines required for accreditation by the National Association for the Education of Young Children (NAEYC, 2007):

| Age | Group size: 6 | Group size: 8 | Group size: 10 | Group size: 12 |
|---|---|---|---|---|
| 12–28 months | 1:3 | 1:4 | 1:4 | 1:4 |
| 21–36 months | | 1:4 | 1:5 | 1:6 |

Problems often encountered in child care centers are staff absences or high staff turnover. Children will be cared for inconsistently and have a hard time bonding to their caregivers if they are cared for by many different people. Consistency is extremely important to toddler development. Being cared for consistently allows toddlers to develop trust (attachment). When a child is confident that his caregiver will always be there when he needs her, he feels more confident in stepping out of his comfort zone to explore his world. This exploration then leads to expanded development of his body and mind.

## Primary Caregiver System

To address issues of consistency, consider a primary caregiver system. Here, one caregiver is assigned to a few children, but she has the support of a team. For example, a group of three caregivers shares a room and works together as a team. Each has three toddlers for whom she is the primary caregiver. Because she is almost always the one responding to her assigned toddlers' needs, each caregiver comes to know the children's temperaments, likes, and dislikes very well. Each has only three children to focus on, so she is able to respond quickly and consistently to each child's needs as they arise. This does not mean that a toddler's primary caregiver is his only caregiver. If a situation develops where a primary caregiver is unable to attend to one of the children, the two other caregivers in the team can work together to attend to the child while still managing the rest of the group. Ideally, a child will have the same primary caregiver throughout his stay at your center. This greatly reduces the stress of yearly transitions for children, family members, and caregivers.

| Primary Caregiver Responsibilities |
| --- |
| ❀ Know the children (likes and dislikes, health issues, developmental stages, temperaments, schedules) |
| ❀ Be a family advocate (sensitive to family culture and values, address family members' needs and concerns) |
| ❀ Facilitate communication (daily communication with family members, update staff on child issues) |

The primary caregiver system has many advantages. It benefits toddlers because it creates a situation in which caregivers can develop strong bonds with their primary children. They learn to understand the individual needs of each child and begin to identify each child's unique way of communicating. When children are responded to quickly and consistently, they learn the important lesson that they can affect their world. A quick and consistent response from a caregiver is not "spoiling" children. Instead, it builds attachment and trust, which are actually critical for healthy toddler independence. It is not uncommon to see toddlers who have developed healthy attachment to their primary caregiver wandering confidently about the room or playground and then "checking in" with their caregiver regularly. A confident toddler will check in either through eye contact or by physically going to the caregiver, saying hello or touching her, and then wandering off again. Caregivers participating in this system also get to know the other children in the group. This group bonding helps the children get some consistency even when their primary caregiver is absent.

Caregivers also benefit from this arrangement. Trying to meet the needs of a busy toddler can be tiring, stressful, and sometimes frustrating. The job is a lot easier when you understand the child's unique behaviors and ways of communicating. Working closely with the same child over a period of time makes it is easier to understand him. Also, caregivers naturally develop positive feelings from bonding with their children, and this makes the work of caregiving more pleasurable. Finally, caregivers working in a team situation have the immediate support of colleagues. Together, they can talk about ideas or concerns and are in a better position to address issues quickly.

Even families benefit from the primary caregiver system. Not only are primary caregivers very familiar with the temperaments and daily activities of the toddlers in their care, they should also be very familiar with the culture and values of their toddlers' families. Primary caregivers are child and family advocates and should inform and update other caregivers and staff on important issues such as medications, cultural beliefs, and other health or family concerns. A team of caregivers can also work together to ensure that each caregiver has a chance to fill out daily communications or to write brief anecdotal records for each child, helping families to stay informed.

## Understanding Toddler Play

In order to create a program that is appropriate for toddlers, it is important to understand toddler play. Toddlers do not play with toys the way preschoolers do. They do not sit and build structures with blocks. Instead, a toddler will carry a block around the room just because he

can. Or he may throw it against a wall to hear the sound it makes. He will not draw a picture with a crayon, but he will hold a crayon and scribble across a paper or any other surface, marveling at the fact that he made a mark! Toddlers' play is not objective oriented. They usually do not have a goal in mind as they begin playing and are not interested in "making" something. They are completely focused on the experience, the act of doing. Their emerging gross and fine motor skills are new and fun to explore. Everything they touch, taste, hear, see, and smell is new and taps into their natural curiosity. When toddlers play, they are simply soaking in the joy of having these new experiences and testing their skills.

A young child at play is simply exploring his surroundings, making choices and new discoveries. Through this unstructured play, a toddler learns about himself (including skills and interests), his world (interacting with people and objects), and problem solving (figuring out how to get the block out from under the couch, how to reach a desired toy, and so on). Your job as a caregiver is to encourage these explorations and to avoid trying to direct or control a toddler's play to make it fit your idea of what play should look like.

# Encouraging Learning

Learning happens when an experience is familiar enough to be understood but new enough to offer exciting challenges. With this in mind, it is easy to see how toddlers at play are constantly encountering learning experiences. They naturally take familiar objects and use them in unexpected ways just to see what will happen. A toddler may notice that a wooden spoon makes a great noise when he bangs on a pot. Next, he may bang the spoon on the floor to see what will happen. From this type of exploration, toddlers learn about the nature of objects, their own physical capabilities, and how to interact with others.

An educational program for toddlers should be based on this natural desire they have to explore and discover. Carefully arrange and plan your toddler environment to encourage free play and problem solving. In this place-based approach to teaching, caregivers may be required to play dramatically different roles than they are used to. Rather than spending the day trying to engage toddlers in activities, such as leading games or directing craft projects, caregivers need to focus on being good child observers.

A good child observer carefully watches toddlers' interactions with the people and objects they encounter throughout the day. It is through these observations that you will learn about the development, skills, and interests of the toddlers in your care. Chances are you will be surprised by all of the new things that you will discover about the children. With this knowledge, you can change or add elements to your environment and set up experiences that will meet the current needs of the toddlers in your care. Most people are amazed to see what long attention spans these young children have when they are truly involved in meaningful play!

Despite the fact that the toddlers in your care are in charge of their own play, planning is still important. Now, instead of spending time planning games or preparing crafts, your time will be spent arranging your environment. Think about the individual needs and interests of each child, and then look at your space with fresh eyes. Ask yourself questions such as, "What objects can I add to encourage exploration or help a child develop a new skill?" "What can I take away because the children are no longer interested?" Create situations in which toddlers can explore objects or challenge their abilities, but allow them to do their own exploring and challenging. Remember, they do it naturally!

Caregivers can also plan experiences for children (experiences that are open-ended, as opposed to activities that generally have a specific desired outcome), but toddlers should be free to choose to participate and to stop participating when they are no longer interested. Also, these experiences should be occasional happenings rather than a constant throughout the day. Look at the following description of a typical activity-based learning environment.

Julie is sitting on the floor, leading the morning circle time song and fingerplay for a group of toddlers. A couple of the children are looking at her with interest, although most are squirming and looking around the room. No one is singing. Marcus, one of the toddlers, suddenly crawls away from the circle time area, heading for a ball that has caught his interest. Another caregiver, Claudia, quickly grabs him and puts him back with group. As she does this, another toddler, Emma, stands up and walks away. Claudia catches up with her and ushers her back to the circle, but the moment she moves away from Marcus, he again heads for the ball he spotted earlier. Julie speeds up the tempo of her song and tries to interest the children by adding a lot of facial expressions and enthusiasm to the fingerplay.

In this scene the caregivers, Julie and Claudia, are taking on the traditional preschool teacher role. Unfortunately, their toddlers are not yet preschoolers. Developmentally, they are not ready to behave as a part of a group. The activity is appropriate for toddlers, but the expectation that all of the children should be engaged and interested at the same time is not. By the time this activity is over, chances are Julie and Claudia will be frustrated, and many of the toddlers will be cranky.

Now take a look at this scene showing a place-based approach. Kim is sitting on the floor watching one of the toddlers in her care, Katie, hammer a ball down its hole in a hammering toy. As the ball disappears, Katie looks at Kim with surprise and asks, "Ball?" Kim replies, telling Katie, "You hit the ball, and it went in the hole." They can hear the ball rolling in the toy until suddenly it appears, and Katie shouts, "Ball!" Kim says, "There's the ball!" as a book is thrust into her face by Dillon, another toddler. Kim asks Dillon if he would like her to read him the book. He nods as he settles into her lap. Katie notices Kim opening the book. She drops her hammer and moves to squeeze into Kim's lap with Dillon. Dillon pushes her away, but Katie is persistent, and in the end they both settle in comfortably. Meanwhile, Jake, another caregiver, has set out some play dough in another part of the room. He is sitting with two children, watching them as they pound and poke their dough. Katie notices this and leaves Kim's lap in the middle of the story to take a closer look. Kim shifts her body to help Katie get up but continues reading to Dillon, who resettles himself in her lap.

Here, toddlers have made choices and have become engaged with objects or people in their environment that interest them. At a glance, it may seem as though these caregivers are not teaching their group, but they have carefully selected the toys and experiences that are available to the children, and through their own explorations, the children are engaged and learning.

## Interacting with Toddlers

Think of the time you spend with the children in your care as being divided into two categories: independent time and in-need time. Independent time is free-play time, a time when children need nothing from their caregiver but attention. While it is important to carefully observe each toddler at play, this does not mean that you should keep your distance. Sit with them. Make yourself available and respond to them. Play when they want you involved, but resist the temptation to always initiate activities. Spending time with a toddler when it does not involve meeting one of his immediate needs helps him to feel valued. It is important quality time.

In-need time is the time you spend with a child attending to his daily care needs. This includes diapering, feeding, dressing, and so on. Do not think of this time as separate from the learning time in your program. This is special one-on-one time that you have with each toddler. While you are changing a child's diaper, talk with him (developing language skills), encourage him to help you (developing self-help, fine, and gross motor skills), and acknowledge his helpfulness (developing social and emotional skills). Daily care experiences are wonderful opportunities for learning! Even young toddlers are quite capable. They can climb sturdy steps to the changing table, feed themselves, and even help set out plates and napkins at snack time. Older toddlers can pour their own drinks using small plastic pitchers and cups, wash their hands, and even clean up their messes with a sponge or small broom. Doing things for themselves is wonderful for toddlers' self-esteem and can also make things easier for you as their caregiver.

| Four Roles of the Caregiver in Toddler Education |
|---|
| ✿ Provide for basic needs and attention: Meet children's basic daily care needs, including the need for attention, without strings attached. |
| ✿ Determine appropriate experiences: Use observation to decide what experiences to make available and whether an experience is too frustrating, too boring, or just right for each child. |
| ✿ Give feedback: Make sure feedback is clear so that children learn the consequences of their actions. |
| ✿ Model good behavior: Behave as you want the children to behave. |

Whether you are engaged in independent or in-need time, interacting with toddlers requires two important skills from you as their caregiver: being a good observer and knowing how to respond. By developing these skills, you can learn to perfect the timing of your interventions. Timing is everything. Remember, toddlers learn best when their abilities are challenged just a little. Having a developmentally appropriate program means making sure children are challenged enough so that they are not bored but not challenged so much that they become frustrated. You can make this happen by carefully observing a child involved in a task and then stepping in when you notice the first signs of frustration. Remember, stepping in does not mean finishing the task for the child. When you do intervene, give only enough help to encourage the child to stick with the problem. Accomplishing a task himself gives a child an enormous feeling of satisfaction and competence, and this will motivate him to work through future problems he encounters.

When you are interacting with a toddler, here are some things to keep in mind:

- ✿ Avoid giving constant praise. Children who receive too much praise no longer feel inner delight in their own accomplishments, but instead look to others for acceptance and external rewards. Instead of saying, "Good job!" try, "Wow, you must feel good about that!"

- ✿ Model the behavior you want to see. Toddlers are wonderful mimics. Mimicking the adults around them is how they learn the complex rules of social behavior. Be aware of how you act or react throughout the day, especially when you are frustrated, angry, or sad. Young children will pick up on this and do as you do.

Of course, not all of your interactions with toddlers will be child initiated. Situations will always arise in which you will need to intervene to keep children safe or to meet their daily care needs. When it is time to change a diaper or serve a snack, try not to disrupt a child who is absorbed in play. Instead, give the child a warning that play will have to end soon, and stick to it. Take the time to involve the child. Tell him what is going on. Too often, toddlers are handled as objects. They are abruptly moved from floor to high chair when it is time to eat or quickly lifted to a standing position without a word when they fall down. Instead, treat a young child as you would an elderly person who needs your assistance. Let him know what you are doing before you do it.

Involving toddlers in their daily care experiences is important, but it is not always easy. As adults and as educators, we want our programs to run smoothly and efficiently. We may feel that it would be faster to carry a child to the changing table than to have him walk. Keep in mind that when you show a toddler that you respect him as an individual, you help to build positive self-esteem and develop a strong relationship.

## Handling "Bad" Behavior

Toddlers' bodies and minds are growing quickly. All of their new abilities give them new independence, but these changes can sometimes be scary. You may see them act very mature one minute, insisting "me do it!" and tackling new tasks. The next minute, they have regressed to behaviors you thought they had outgrown. Toddlers are emotionally complex. They require a lot of individual attention and are very sensitive to your opinions of them. The physical and emotional stresses they experience as they move from being babies to becoming capable children are actually very similar to those experienced by teenagers. Expect them to be moody, and try to be understanding.

As toddlers begin to develop a sense of self, they test boundaries. Young children test boundaries to make sure they are there. As frustrating as this can be to caregivers and family members, asserting independence is a healthy and important part of toddler development. You can lessen the frustration by being consistent. It is through consistency that young children learn about your expectations.

Another way to make this boundary testing easier on you and the toddlers in your care is to set up your environment in a way that ensures off-limits places are truly off-limits. For example, installing a gate to block a toddler's access to stairs will prevent you from having to pull him off of the stairs constantly. Ensure that everything in your toddler space can be safely explored by toddlers. Remove anything that they should not touch, and always be clear and consistent with the limits you impose.

Like younger infants, a toddler's bad behavior may be a sign that he has a need that is not being met. He may be tired, hungry, need more attention from you, or feel overstimulated. Try to identify and fulfill these needs.

Toddlers may also act out when they do not know how to express their feelings. They may feel angry that a toy was taken away by another child or hurt when their family member leaves for the day. Help children to identify these feelings. Validate them and show children healthy ways to express them.

No matter what the source of the toddler's behavior problems, punishment does not belong in a toddler environment. Calm persistence and consistency are much more successful ways of changing behavior. If this does not work, or if the situation calls for more direct action, firm but gentle physical restraint is appropriate. For example, if Eliza is about to hit Noah on the head with a block, firmly grab Eliza's arm and gently remove the block as you explain to her that she was going to hurt Noah. Avoid shaming or belittling young children. They are learning the rules of society. Social skills do not come naturally. These skills develop through instruction and experiences.

No matter how frustrated you may feel by a toddler's behavior, always talk to him calmly, and never try to control him with your anger. Young children are excellent mimics. Watching your behavior is one of the ways they learn. If you try to control a child with anger, it is very likely that he will try to do the same to you. Here are a few ideas on how to handle common toddler behavior issues.

# Oppositional Behavior

Oppositional behavior is when a child consistently says no, ignores you, or does the opposite of what you want him to do.

- ✿ Help toddlers to identify and express their feelings. Ask, "Are you feeling angry? If you feel angry, tell me with words. Just say, 'I am mad!'"

- ✿ Tell children how you feel about specific behaviors. "I understand that you are angry. That is okay. But it is not okay to scream at me and hit me. It hurts, and I do not like it."

- ✿ Get playful. Ask many silly questions to give toddlers opportunities to say no; for example, ask, "Do we eat bicycles for breakfast?"

## Biting

Observe a child carefully to identify why he bites. Is he teething? Experimenting? Exploring cause and effect? Maybe he is asserting his independence, asking for attention, or imitating behavior. He may feel frustrated or threatened. The strategies you use to address this behavior will vary greatly depending on the cause.

- ✿ Offer teething toys or teething biscuits for the child to mouth.

- ✿ Reinforce positive social behaviors, giving children attention for the good things they do.

- ✿ Provide many opportunities for social interaction in very small groups. Give guidance as needed.

- ✿ Watch for signs of rising frustration, and intervene.

- ✿ Offer positive alternatives to biting. Model supportive behavior. Never bite a child to show how it feels to be bitten!

- ✿ Give extra attention regularly throughout the day.

- ✿ Provide many sensory and motor experiences.

## Tantrums

Toddlers are just learning about their emotions. They may not fully understand what they are feeling and why. Temper tantrums are as unpleasant for the child as they are for the adult. They often leave toddlers exhausted and probably even frightened by

their loss of control. Once a tantrum starts, there is not much you can do but try to keep the child (and other children) safe, but here are some suggestions for preventing or at least minimizing tantrums.

Minimize frustrations by setting up your environment in a way that allows children to explore without your having to constantly police them.

- ✿ Make sure toys match the abilities of children. Have familiar, "easy," or "comfort" toys handy for children having a bad day.

- ✿ Give children many opportunities to feel competent. Ask them to help with daily chores.

- ✿ Offer choices. If a child does not want to go outside, give him two choices of activities or toys you know he enjoys outdoors. You are still getting him outdoors, but now he feels more in control because he feels the choice was his.

- ✿ Give toddlers a chance to be hugged and cuddled. While they love being "big kids," they often long to feel like babies again, too.

- ✿ Anticipate physical needs; for example, serve lunch before children get too hungry, or transition them to nap time before they are too tired.

## Dealing with Separation Anxiety

Saying goodbye in the morning can be a very difficult time for toddlers and their family members. You may not always approve of the way a family member handles these goodbyes, but it is important to respect family members' feelings and the family culture. Whether it is a long goodbye or short and sweet, here are some recommendations to pass along to families, and guidelines for you to follow:

- ✿ Always say goodbye: Sneaking out on a child can cause him to be fearful and lose trust.

- ✿ Once a goodbye is said, the family member should depart immediately: A long goodbye process is fine, but lingering after the actual goodbye sends confusing mixed messages to the child.

- ✿ Allow children to experience their feelings: Do not deny a child his feelings by telling him not to cry, that mommy will be back. Instead, acknowledge his sadness and let him express it.

- ✿ Have something ready to interest the child: Once the child's feelings have been acknowledged and he has had an opportunity to express them, give him a special toy or point out something that will interest him, and help him move into the routine of the day.

# Involving Families

Quality child care programs serve not only children but their families as well. Parenting a young child can be difficult and stressful. Some family members may be first-time parents, inexperienced with young children and overwhelmed by the demands of a toddler or stressed by the financial burden of a child. Others may be dealing with complicated issues of sibling rivalry or balancing work and family.

It is also common for family members to have mixed emotions about leaving their child in the care of others. They may feel guilty or concerned about whether their child's needs will be met while they are away. Some family members may feel uncomfortable in a child care setting, not knowing how to act. They may see you as an expert on children and may feel intimidated. All family members need to feel that they are part of their child's day even when they cannot physically be there. This connection is not only important for families, it is also important for the child. It is up to you to make that happen.

As a caregiver, you have to perform a balancing act. Family members want to feel that you are competent, but they do not want to feel that you know more about how to care for their child than they do. They want their child to like you and enjoy going to child care, but they do not want to feel that their child likes you more than them. Families want to know what their child does each day, but some families may not want to hear that they missed their child's first word or other important milestones. You can address these concerns by being sensitive to these potentially conflicting feelings. Instead of announcing that their child said the word *more* today, consider asking families to listen for the word because you thought you may have heard it. Be supportive and reassuring to family members. These mixed feelings are normal and go hand in hand with sharing care. Let them know that they are the most important people in their child's life.

| To help family members feel at ease, welcome, and involved, think about the following aspects of your program: |
| --- |
| ✿ The entrance: Is it welcoming and comfortable? |
| ✿ The toddler area: Does it include and reflect the children's families and cultures? Does it encourage families to sit and watch their toddlers at play? |
| ✿ Communication: Do family members receive a consistent and accurate idea of how their child's day has been? How do they learn about upcoming events or get information about parenting issues? |

The entrance and the toddler area of your program really do set the tone and visually reinforce the values of your program. However, they will be discussed more in the next section of this book. Here, we will give you ideas on how to communicate with family members in a way that makes them feel involved.

The best way to really communicate with family members is to talk with them one-on-one. However, the end of the day is always hectic, and talking with each family member is easier said than done. One simple way to communicate the basics of each child's day is to have a clipboard for each child, with a chart that can be filled out easily by the primary caregiver. You will find two examples of these charts at the end of this section. Make these charts easily accessible to caregivers during the day, and then hang them in the same place each afternoon so that family members can access them easily as well. Family members in a rush to pick up their child can have a quick look to see how the day went. Those who have more time can have a look at their child's chart as they wait for you to become available to answer a question, address a concern, or just talk. Create some sort of a system to keep track of which family members you have spoken with. Make sure to have one-on-one conversations with each family member on a regular basis. Keep these daily charts in each child's file for future reference (refer to the chart on page 25). They can come in handy if you ever need to identify a behavior pattern in the future.

Another great way to make families feel a part of your program is to take a lot of photographs. Unlike the daily charts, photographs capture the spirit of your program. Display the pictures in the entrance and in other areas. These photos are a great way to draw in apprehensive family members and to get busy families to slow down for a moment. All family members love to see that their children are engaged and happy while they are away. This can be especially helpful to people who have difficulty with separation. Be sure to change the pictures often. Toddlers grow quickly, and you want to send the signal that your program is fresh and current.

## Daily Chart

| Name | Date |
|------|------|
|      |      |

| I had a great time | I need more |
|---|---|
|   |   |

| I ate ◯ all of my lunch<br>◯ about half of my lunch<br>◯ some of my lunch | I enjoyed my bottles or snacks.<br>a.m. _____<br>p.m. _____ |

| I napped<br>a.m. _____<br>a.m. _____<br>p.m. _____<br>p.m. _____ | I had diaper changes.<br>a.m. _____<br>a.m. _____<br>p.m. _____<br>p.m. _____<br><br>I had potty time.<br>a.m. _____<br>a.m. _____<br>p.m. _____<br>p.m. _____ |

## Daily Update

**Child's Name** _____

**Date** _____

| A NOTE FROM FAMILY MEMBERS | | |
|---|---|---|
| Today you can reach me: | ○ at the usual number | ○ at this number |
| Last night my child slept: | ○ very well <br> ○ well | ○ less than usual <br> ○ more than usual |

| | | |
|---|---|---|
| So far my child's mood has been: | | |
| The last feeding was at: | | |
| Special instructions or things to be aware of today include: | | |
| My child will be picked up at: | ○ the usual time | ○ by |

| A NOTE FROM CAREGIVERS | | |
|---|---|---|
| Today your child has been feeling: | | |
| Your baby enjoyed: | | |
| At lunch your child ate: | ○ everything <br> ○ some things | ○ most things <br> ○ very little |
| Snacks today were: | given at <br> given at | |
| Just to let you know: | | |
| Naps | Bottles | Diaperings |

# Chapter 2: Creating Your Environment

The environment of a quality toddler program is more than the arrangement of furniture and the selection of toys. A quality environment encourages family involvement, ensures that children are safe, and supports children's development. A well-thought-out space makes it easy for caregivers to spend quality time with individuals. It is the visual expression of all that your program stands for.

A place-based program is a wonderful way to meet individual children's needs on their own schedules. It means that the furniture, arrangement of space, available toys, and materials are all carefully planned so toddlers learn as they interact with their environment. Each child is able to develop skills and have new experiences at her own pace as she makes her way through the day. In this sort of a classroom, you will seldom find all of the children doing the same thing at the same time. Children will be making their own choices about which of the carefully planned play elements placed about the room they are going to explore and for how long. Special activities or experiences are often a planned part of the day, but they do not take place at a specific "activity time," and children are not required to participate. Instead, these planned experiences are simply set out for the children to explore throughout the day. If the selected activities require adult support, they can be made available during a chunk of time that fits with the rhythm of your day.

# Welcoming

Your entrance is your program's first impression. It is the first thing that family members see and the one area of your program that family members will enter every day. As a result, this space should be family friendly. Consider displaying photos in this space of the children in your program both engaged in activities and with their families. This sends family members the message that you value their child's daily experiences and that you value families as well.

The entrance is also a great place to encourage communication with family members. Hang a clipboard for each child at eye level where family members can review their child's daily chart. If wall space is an issue, consider a box of hanging files, one per child, where family members can find daily charts and other communications such as newsletters or parenting tips and information.

| Learning environments should do the following: |
| --- |
| ✿ Promote all areas of development (language, sensory, social, emotional, cognitive, and motor) |
| ✿ Encourage a positive self-concept and support home cultures |
| ✿ Encourage positive social interactions |
| ✿ Promote diversity and avoid racial or gender stereotypes |

The entrance is also likely to be the site of many hellos and goodbyes. If your space is large enough, you may want to include a comfortable chair or two where family members can sit with their child to say goodbye or take a moment to snuggle before heading back home at the end of the day. Cubbies for children's personal items and a counter or bench where family members can dress and undress children are also useful.

In addition to the entrance, several other indoor spaces will make up your program. These will vary from program to program but should include a food preparation and eating area, a sleeping area, a diapering and toileting area, an active play area, and a quiet play area. These may be defined by existing walls or by the arrangement of low shelves or other furniture. Lofts at a height appropriate for toddlers are another great way to define an area. Not only do they provide a separate, secluded space, but they give children a new vantage point from which to view the room as well.

A toddler environment should be designed on two levels, one below three feet that meets the needs of children, the other above to meet the needs of adults. It is a good idea to get down on the floor every now and then and look at your space from a toddler's perspective. No matter what you use to define your environment, make sure that children can be easily observed and spaces easily accessed by caregivers. To prevent toddlers from spending the day wandering aimlessly through your program space, consider setting up motor challenges at the entrances of some areas. An entrance that challenges toddlers to step up or crawl through is great for motor development.

As you are defining your areas, here are some tips to make them successful.

- ✿ Set up your space to require few rules: Make off-limits areas inaccessible to toddlers, and make sure that everything is touchable and mouthable.

- ✿ Avoid overstimulation: Limit the number of toys on shelves, pictures on walls, and objects in and around cribs or changing tables. You want your space to be visually pleasing, not overwhelming.

- ✿ Think about how space affects behavior: Large, open areas encourage active exploration and physical movement. Small spaces encourage concentration and social interaction.

- ✿ Think about maintenance: Make sure the floor under eating and other messy areas can be easily cleaned and that the surfaces that children will crawl upon are soft and also easily cleaned. Organize and label storage space.

- ✿ Think about staff comfort: Provide comfortable seating with back support for adults to sit with young children, and make sure that cribs and changing tables are at a comfortable height.

Both behavior and mood can be greatly influenced by our physical environment, so it is important that the space you create be visually pleasing to both caregivers and children. Display pictures at child height. A low fish tank can be soothing and entertaining to young children. No matter how you fill your space, remember, too much stimulation can be overwhelming or make toddlers passive observers who demand entertainment rather than being actively involved in their environment.

## Meeting Needs

### Food Area

Whether your food area includes a complete kitchen or simply a microwave, sink, and small fridge, make sure you have low tables and chairs and child-sized utensils. Meal times are a great opportunity for toddlers to exert their independence. The more independent toddlers can be when eating, the easier it will be on you. Plastic (nonbreakable) dishes, cups, and small pitchers, which encourage toddlers to pour their own drinks, are also important. Have plenty of paper towels and sponges handy for small spills, and consider comfortable chairs for adults. Keep this area organized by including ample storage and by labeling items. This area should be located in a space with an easily washable floor.

### Sleeping Area

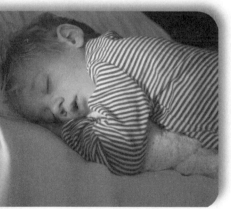

If you have the space to create a separate sleeping area, make sure you place it in the quietest spot possible and paint it with calming colors. Programs with less space can pull out mats or portable cots to use at nap time. Arrange them far enough apart so that children will not disturb one another, and try to position them away from toy shelves or other distractions. Be sure to store these mats in an area that is out of the way yet easily accessible to caregivers. Allowing children to snuggle with special toys and blankets from home can help to encourage napping. These items will also need storage space. Consider using soothing music or a little water fountain to create a restful atmosphere. The sleeping area should also include rockers or other chairs that enable adults to cuddle and soothe children.

### Diapering Area

Make sure this area is near a sink or bathroom. Include sturdy steps that allow toddlers to climb up to changing tables. This encourages independence and will save a lot of strain on caregivers' backs. Some toddlers are very active, squirming constantly on the changing table, so it is important to keep items such as diapers, wipes, and the diaper-disposal bin within easy reach. You may want to include a large, wall-mounted mirror positioned for children to look into, or post an engaging picture on the ceiling. Consider having a few easy-to-clean toys handy as well to keep active hands busy. Diapering is an excellent opportunity for caregivers to give quality one-on-one time, and sometimes your focused attention and a little conversation are all a toddler needs to settle down for a diaper change.

## Toileting Area

This area should have step stools for toilets, or low toilets and potty chairs. Sinks should also be low or provide sturdy steps up to an adult-sized sink. Soap and paper towels should be within easy reach for toddlers. Place waste baskets in convenient locations. Rebus charts or posters that remind children of the steps for toileting and washing hands, posted at toddler-eye level, can also be useful. Because most toddlers will need your help as they learn to use the toilet, consider replacing a standard door with a half-door. This will give more independent toddlers privacy while allowing you to keep an eye on them.

# Exploring and Playing

Much of your space will be dedicated to encouraging the toddlers in your care to play and explore. While in your program, children need an opportunity to be active and loud. They also need to be able to escape from the noise and activity and have opportunities to engage in quiet play. Your spaces will need to accommodate all of these needs. One effective way to ensure that toddlers have the opportunity to explore and engage all areas of development as they play in your space is by creating exploration centers.

## Exploration Centers

Many preschool programs divide their spaces into distinct activity areas or learning centers. While the focus of these centers may be different, this concept also works well in a toddler environment. Here are some advantages of learning centers:

✿ Materials are more likely to be found, used, and put away because they are kept in or near the area where they will most likely be used.

✿ Children are more likely to spread out as they take advantage of different centers of interest.

✿ Children are able to see the variety of new activities or experiences they can choose to engage in.

✿ Children are more likely to stay focused on an activity of their choosing.

When using the learning-center concept with toddlers, the centers you choose to provide should be designed to encourage the exploration of specific skills or areas of development. For example, you could have a gross motor center where children can climb, jump, slide, and crawl. In a sensory center, children can explore different textures or smells, discover mirrors, and play with colors. At a dressing center, children can practice putting on slippers, unzipping zippers, or trying on skirts and capes.

The location of any center that you create is important and deserves careful thought. A gross motor center will need a lot of space, while a book nook should be in a small, quiet area. If you set the two centers next to each other, your quiet space is not going to be very successful. Some centers can go anywhere; others have specific needs. For example, an art center should be near a sink and over a floor surface that can be washed easily. Once you have an idea of the types of centers you would like to provide and where each will go, use low shelves, climbing structures, and other furniture to define and separate each space.

With your exploration centers in place, the next step is deciding which materials to set out. The amount of materials you make available will depend on the size of the center and the available child-accessible storage. Toddlers can become overwhelmed by too many choices, so be selective about what you offer. Observe the children carefully as they explore each center, and pay attention to which items they choose. If something is not being used, remove it and replace it with something else. You can also change up the centers based on themes or areas of interest. One week the sensory center may be full of bubble wrap, crinkled craft paper, and other textured materials, and the next week you may put those away and set out scoops and a bin of coffee grounds mixed with sand. Inevitably, different children will choose to play with and explore different materials depending on their interests and abilities.

Even in the most well-thought-out learning center environment, materials are likely to wander. Carrying things from place to place is just what toddlers love to do! When children are finished using an item, encourage them to put it away, but avoid controlling children's movement. Positive experiences should be encouraged wherever they spontaneously occur. Be flexible and expect nothing more than that toddlers will be toddlers.

| Learning center areas to consider for toddlers: |
| --- |
| ✿ Water Play: explore bubbles and sensory and dramatic play experiences |
| ✿ Book Nook: investigate board books, soft books, and other text formats |
| ✿ Climbing: climb over, under, and through sturdy items |
| ✿ Mirror: examine low, shatterproof mirrors |
| ✿ Blocks: build, fill, and dump blocks of all shapes, sizes, and textures |
| ✿ Dramatic Play: imitate life at home, school, store, and so on |
| ✿ Costume: explore hats, scarves, and other dress-up items |
| ✿ Action Center: investigate busy boxes, sorting boxes, pounding toys, and other activities |
| ✿ Sound: experiment with instruments, sound-making toys, and recording devices |
| ✿ Animals: explore, including live animals, stuffed animals, plastic animals, and pictures of animals |
| ✿ Art: experience play dough, finger paints, sticky paper collage, and other art activities |

## Active Play

Toddlers are active explorers, excited about exploring their developing motor skills whether they are indoors or out, and so it is important that you include an active play area within your classroom space. A good indoor active play environment for toddlers should look more like a vibrant gym or obstacle course than a classroom. Be sure to include obstacles that children can climb over, under, and through. Provide a variety of surface textures and spaces to explore. Thick mats can be stacked to create low steps or platforms that children can climb up. Carpet-covered low steps or platforms also work well. Other wonderful additions to a toddler indoor play space include large cubes or blocks, tunnels, slides, riding toys, and large cardboard boxes to crawl in

CREATING YOUR ENVIRONMENT

and out of. Toddlers will use low tables, bookshelves, or any other furniture to climb and pull up on, so make sure that everything is sturdy and will not topple. Also, provide both hard and soft surfaces for toddlers to crawl and walk across. If you have wall-to-wall carpeting, lay some linoleum squares or bamboo mats on top of it. Place several area rugs over a hard floor.

Choice is important, so provide a variety of toys on low, sturdy shelves or in open bins that children can access easily. Be conscious of the amount of toys you set out. Too many can be overwhelming, and too much clutter can make it hard to move around. To a toddler, a bin full of toys is an invitation to play fill-and-dump games. Instead, select a few toys, and put them out on open shelves that children can access easily. Great active toys for toddlers include soft balls, push toys, cars, and carts. Toddlers also love exploring materials to sort, match, fit together, and arrange. If you have a lot of toys, consider rotating them. This will reduce cleanup and clutter, and you will see the children's excitement when they discover that you have brought out new toys. It is always a good idea to keep a few favorites for the children who like the security of toys they can count on.

## Quiet Time

In addition to testing their bodies physically, the toddlers in your care are going to need opportunities to rest, snuggle up, or explore quietly. Have plenty of cushions and comfortable places for both adults and toddlers to sit, snuggle, and read. Cozy nooks under lofts or other small, semi-enclosed spaces where toddlers can go to "tune out" the world are especially nice to have for those children who are easily overstimulated. Your quiet play space should have a calm and soothing atmosphere. Consider playing soft, soothing music to calm children. Cover overhead lights with tinted transparency paper or sheer, flame-retardant fabric (do not do this if light fixtures are prone to getting hot).

When you bring together soft music, pillows, fuzzy blankets or rugs, and dim lighting, you are giving cues to all of the senses that this is a space to be calm and quiet. In this quiet space, you can set out books, lacing beads, puzzles, and other quiet activities. Toddlers can also enjoy quiet time outdoors. Set out blankets and pillows to encourage children to sit back and relax.

## Outdoor Space

Spending time outdoors is also important for the health and emotional well-being of the children and should be a part of your daily routine. The outdoors is not only a great place to let out extra energy, it can provide wonderful opportunities for learning as well, so be sure to give your outdoor space as much thought as your indoor space. When taking young children outside, consider the following.

Young toddlers love to cruise and explore the outdoors. For them, include safe, low obstacles for crawling and climbing. Riding toys and outdoor play equipment sized for toddlers are also great. But to really make the most of children's outdoor experiences, include natural and found items such as logs, rocks, and tree stumps. They bring an important natural element into your outdoor space and are wonderful objects to pull up on, crawl over, straddle, and explore.

A sandbox can provide wonderful sensory and motor experiences, and low seat-style swings are always exciting for toddlers. A fun alternative to a low toddler swing is a porch swing. Here caregivers can sit with toddlers while they swing, or swing them gently as they sit

| Toys to promote gross motor skills | |
|---|---|
| push-pull toys | tumbling mats |
| riding toys | balls |
| rocking toys | scarves |
| beanbags | vinyl-covered foam |
| wagons | furniture |
| climbers and slides | |
| Toys to promote fine motor skills | |
| interlocking blocks | puzzles (3–8 pieces) |
| large beads and shoelaces | containers to dump and fill |
| busy boxes | shape sorters |
| stacking rings | |

CREATING YOUR ENVIRONMENT

supported by the swing's back. Remember, no matter what type of swing you provide, never leave a toddler unattended in a swing!

Also keep in mind that young children have sensitive skin, so be sure to have ample shade in your outdoor area or otherwise protect the children. No matter how enclosed or safe you feel your outdoor play area is, check the area frequently to make sure that it is free of glass, nails, pesticides, and other things that may cause harm. Finally, be sure to have some comfortable seating for caregivers as well.

# Chapter 3: Planning Your Program

Program planning includes all of the elements of your program that are not related to your room and furniture. When planning your toddler program, remember this: *Child care environments are not schools; they are places to live.*

Good homes are the best models for infant and toddler care. Good homes give children a sense of belonging. Learning experiences occur every day as children help their family members with tasks and watch older children. Time is basically unscheduled. Events and activities are constantly popping up, but in a natural, unscheduled way. Everything is explorable because family members have taken the time to childproof everything. Children are being watched, but they have the freedom to move about on their own terms and find quiet, solitary places if they feel the need. In general, a good home is a place where children can enjoy their childhood feeling supported, safe, carefree, and unscheduled.

## Grouping Young Children

Infants and toddlers are not very small preschoolers. They are little people at unique stages of development, completely self-focused and constantly testing their abilities and boundaries. They are not developmentally ready to be in large groups. The numbers that make up a large group are also relative depending on children's ages. Below are recommended child-to-caregiver ratios according to the National Association for the Education of Young Children accreditation standards (NAEYC, 2007): These guidelines are for NAEYC program accreditation only. It is important that you check on the legal requirements of your state before grouping children.

| Age | Group size | Child-to-staff ratio |
|---|---|---|
| Birth to 15 months | 6 | 3:1 |
| | 8 | 4:1 |
| 12–28 months: same as above plus . . . | 10 | 4:1 |
| | 12 | 4:1 |
| 21–36 months | 10 | 5:1 |
| | 12 | 6:1 |

We discussed this chart earlier as we explored the importance of helping toddlers and their caregivers bond, and it is also a useful guide as you explore your options for grouping children. The decision to use a primary caregiver system is a separate issue from how you group the toddlers in your care, and this system works with any grouping style.

As important as a good child-to-caregiver ratio may be, it is not the only consideration when deciding how to group the toddlers in your program. Their ages, developmental stages, and needs are also important, as are the interests and skills of your staff. Your program space will also impact grouping. You may legally be able to put 12 toddlers in a room with three staff, but if your space is broken up into very small rooms, you might want to consider creating smaller groups. There are many ways to group young children, including mixed-age grouping, same-age grouping, and flexible-age grouping.

## Mixed-Age Grouping

Mixed-age grouping is how children are naturally grouped in families and has many advantages. It can be less stressful for children than same-age grouping because it honors their individual differences. Caregivers naturally expect children of different ages to have different abilities and interests. While we all know this to be true, in same-age grouping, there is a strong temptation to compare children and to have all children doing the same thing at the same time.

In mixed-age groups, older children interact with younger children, playing, helping, and watching one another. Being more skilled and independent than the others in their group boosts older children's confidence. Younger children also benefit. They learn new skills and are motivated to try new things by watching and playing with their older friends. Another advantage to mixed-age groups is that siblings can be grouped together. This can be a great benefit for families. Often in mixed-age groupings, the group (caregivers and children) stays the same over a period of years, creating a more stable environment for children.

There are some disadvantages to mixed-age grouping. Grouping children of different ages together may be restricted by your state's child care guidelines. Some caregivers may prefer to focus their attention on one particular age or developmental stage. And because some states (and NAEYC accreditation guidelines) require that the child-to-caregiver ratio be in compliance with the age of the youngest member of the group, mixed-age grouping can also be more expensive.

## Same-Age Grouping

Same-age grouping has some advantages for staff. It is easier to put children on the same schedule (though this is not always best for the children). It is easier to ensure that all of the materials that children can access are developmentally appropriate. Some caregivers may prefer same-age grouping because they are more comfortable with, or drawn to, a particular developmental stage. Family members may be more comfortable with same-age groups out of concern that, in mixed-age groups, older children may harm their infants or that younger children may hinder the development of older children. Most experts agree that this concern is unfounded.

The primary disadvantage of same-age grouping for children is that they are often removed from a familiar group at a time dictated by the calendar and not based on their needs. When children change groups, their caregiver often changes as well, which can be unsettling for toddlers and works against caregiver bonding. This can be addressed by having caregivers follow the same group of children up through the years.

## Flexible-Age Grouping

Flexible-age grouping combines some of the elements of same-age grouping with mixed-age grouping. Here, children are put into groups based on natural developmental breaks. The range of ages is not as wide as with mixed-age grouping, but it is wide enough to allow younger children to learn from older children. Flexible-age grouping is also good for caregivers because they do not have to manage a full spectrum of developmental abilities. However, there is enough variety in developmental stages that children are not competing for the same resources. Many program administrators find this grouping helpful because it reduces the stress both caregivers and children experience when the calendar indicates a child should be moved to the next room but space is not available. Following is one example of flexible-grouping age ranges:

- 6 weeks to 15 months (limited language and not walking consistently)
- 12 months to 30 months (developing language and walking)
- 24 months to 36 months (proficient language)

No matter which method of grouping you choose, you can create a more cohesive environment among all of the children and staff if you encourage mixed-age experiences in small groups on a regular basis. These could be at lunchtime, during outdoor play, or for special activities.

## Creating a Schedule

When thinking about a daily schedule for toddler programs, one golden rule holds true: the younger the child, the more flexible and individualized the schedule needs to be. As a caregiver, you need to provide consistency but also more than a touch of flexibility. A predictable schedule will help a toddler feel more secure. However, being flexible in that schedule will help you to meet the immediate needs of individual toddlers that are sure to arise. Having some flexibility can also help you to take advantage of unplanned learning experiences.

To meet these seemingly opposing needs, consider a schedule based on events rather than on time. Individual toddlers generally come to your program with their own internal schedule already set. They wake up, have a diaper change, and eat. They may play for a bit independently while their family dresses and gets ready for the day and follow that up with family play time or a morning outing. Then, it is time for their mid-morning nap, another diaper change, and it is play time again, and so on. Consider basic care elements when establishing your daily schedule:

- Arrivals and departures
- Feeding and food preparation (meals and snacks)
- Diapering and toileting
- Sleeping
- Dressing (transitions to and from the outdoors)

Aside from meeting a toddler's basic needs, a daily schedule should also include the following:

- ✿ Active play time and quiet, cuddling times

- ✿ Time with others, time alone, and one-on-one time

- ✿ Child-chosen activities and those offered by adults

- ✿ Indoor and outdoor play experiences

Remember, your program needs to fit the child, not the other way around. Learn as much as you can about each child's home schedule, and try to remain compatible with it. Gather information from families about children's home routines, and think about the fixed elements of your program, including pickup and drop-off times, lunch, staff breaks, and so on. Then put together the various elements to create a schedule that best fits everyone's needs. Here is a sample toddler schedule for a full-day program:

- ✿ Arrival and undressing (outerwear)

- ✿ Welcome routine

- ✿ Active exploration and learning centers

- ✿ Dressing (outerwear)

- ✿ Outdoor time

- ✿ Undressing (outerwear)

- ✿ Lunch

- ✿ Nap

- ✿ Quiet activities

- ✿ Dressing (outerwear)

- ✿ Outdoor time

- ✿ Undressing (outerwear)

- ✿ Goodbye routine

- ✿ Dismissal and dressing (outerwear)

Notice, there are no times posted on this schedule. If the children are very engaged in their own explorations at the learning centers, that block could take most of the morning. If they are having difficulties focusing, or if conflicts between children seem to be on the rise, consider shortening that exploration time and heading outside early.

You may also notice that diapering and snack are not included in this schedule. Most toddlers struggle with transitions. Rather than scheduling in a diapering time, check in with the children frequently, and change them as needed. Instead of a snack time, consider setting up a small snack table where a few small portions of the day's snack are made available to children as needed. A child can let you know she wants a snack simply by sitting at the table. This does require some extra monitoring by caregivers, but in a primary caregiver system where one person is especially in tune with the needs of only a few children, bringing the day's snack to the snack table when a child chooses to sit at the table is not especially burdensome, and it does reduce the number of transitions that a child experiences throughout the day.

This schedule includes a welcome and goodbye routine. Use a short routine that you do with all children as they arrive or leave, such as a one- or two-line song, a hug, and a quick sign-in and sign-out procedure (placing the child's photo on a felt board, putting away belongings, and so on). This routine can also be done as an optional large-group activity. Any time you plan a large-group activity for toddlers, make sure that it is short and optional. Have choices available for those children who lose interest or do not want to participate. These routines help children transition into and out of your program.

When you have decided on a schedule that works for your program, consider posting a pictorial version in a place where children, families, and staff can see it easily. Include pictures representing daily care activities as well. The toddlers in your care cannot read this schedule, but it can be a helpful tool to guide them through their day and build their language skills.

Even nonverbal toddlers can learn to communicate through pictures. With the help of this visual schedule, a toddler can ask for snack time, let you know she needs a diaper change, or express a desire to go outside. Visual cues and tools, like a visual schedule, can cut down on a lot of the frustrations that arise when a toddler cannot communicate her needs or desires. Posting a schedule also helps to keep all of your staff aware and up-to-date on the anticipated order of events for the day and keeps families informed as well.

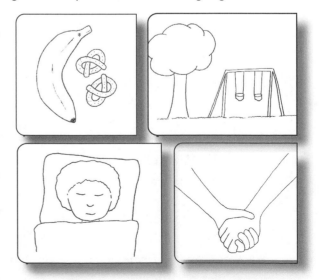

No matter how you put together the elements of your schedule, be sure to move through the day at a child's pace. The toddlers in your care are not thinking about what is going to happen next; they are focused on the "now." Planning ahead and being prepared will help you to focus on the "now," too. Enjoy the toddlers' experiences, and do not rush them on to the next activity.

## Planning

The daily schedule is the skeleton of your program. Planning is what fleshes it out. Planning ahead, short-term and long-term, will help you to be sure that you are meeting the needs of each child. It will also ensure that the children have many varied and enriching experiences that support their development. Current brain research shows that early experiences help to form important pathways in young children's brains, laying the foundation for future learning.

Like every other aspect of your toddler program, planning here is very different from planning in a preschool classroom. Instead of planning activities with a particular end result, think about planning open-ended experiences. To do so, you need to put a lot of thought into your environment. For example, you may decide that some of the toddlers in your care need more practice with fine motor skills. Instead of planning an activity where toddlers will color a page in a coloring book, you can encourage fine motor development by adding sponges and brushes to the water play area. With this hands-on experience, some toddlers can explore the fine motor skills required to squeeze a sponge, while others will enjoy pushing the sponge underwater and watching it bounce up. Different children will practice and develop different skills and concepts with the same activity. That is what makes it open ended.

Sometimes you may want to plan a specific activity; but when doing so, focus on the child's experience and not the end product. Finger paints and other art activities can provide enriching sensory experiences. Toddlers will explore the feel of the paints on their fingers, marvel at the marks they can make on the paper, and then be amazed when another pass of the hand changes those marks. They are not the least bit interested in making something that looks nice. Most children will not pay much attention to what they are making until they are three years old, so avoid activities that ask toddlers to create a specific finished product.

PLANNING YOUR PROGRAM

Language development is especially important during the toddler years. Toddlers are learning to put together sounds to make words and are eager to learn the words for the objects and people in their environment. They are excited about communicating and need a lot of opportunities to be exposed to and explore language. For this reason, it is important to think about how you are going to provide rich language experiences every day. This can be done in many ways:

✿ Reading books: When you read with toddlers you are introducing new words and ideas that build vocabulary. You are also introducing basic concepts of print such as how to hold a book and turn pages, and the idea that books communicate stories or information.

✿ Storytelling: Making up stories and sharing them with children develops listening skills, promotes creative thinking and visualizing, and builds vocabulary. Storytelling is especially good for personalizing the language experience. You can adjust the length and complexity of the story based on the development of the individual child, and you can make the stories personally relevant to children, helping to develop language and vocabulary that relates to each child's life experiences and cultural background.

✿ Songs and rhymes: Traditional songs, nursery rhymes, and silly songs and rhymes that you create all help children to understand that words are created by putting together different sounds. This sound (or phonemic) awareness is the foundation for speech and for reading.

All successful planning relies on two things: observation and evaluation. Watch the children carefully. Where are they each developmentally? What are their likes and dislikes? When are they more apt to be open to new experiences, and when are they fussier?

Next, take a look at your program's general goals and objectives. Are you doing enough to support each toddler as an individual? Keep daily anecdotal records (notes describing the child, what she is doing, how she reacts to a situation) to help you monitor your effectiveness. The idea of record keeping may sound daunting, especially when toddlers keep you on your toes all day long. But when you take the time each day to write about each child, even if it is just once sentence, you will gain great insight into behavior patterns, skills, and interests that you

| Important Program Goals and Objectives for Toddlers |
| --- |
| 1. To feel valued, competent, and supported |
| 2. To express feelings appropriately |
| 3. To develop positive relationships with adults and peers |
| 4. To learn to communicate (verbally and nonverbally) |
| 5. To develop motor and self-help skills |
| 6. To develop thinking skills |
| 7. To experience consistency between home and caregiver environments |

might not have noticed otherwise. Once you are clear on each child's developmental stage, emotional needs, skills, and interests, planning experiences that are engaging and that support the toddlers' development should be easy.

At least once a month, make a note of the new goals and objectives you have for each child, as toddlers grow and change quickly. Remember, goals are more long-term, and objectives are the small steps you take to reach those goals. When you have gotten an idea of an experience you would like to provide to support one of these goals, write it down. Create a to-do list delineating materials you will need and noting any changes you will need to make to your environment. The more you have done ahead of time, the more smoothly things will go and the more time you will have to enjoy each experience with the toddlers in your care. Most important, be flexible. You may be excited to introduce them to soap bubbles, but if the day comes and several of the children are fussy or not feeling well, the experience will probably be more successful if you wait for another day. The toddlers' moods are not the only variables that might cause you to alter your plans. Consider unexpected events and your own mood as well.

## Transitions

Transitioning toddlers from one task, event, or activity to another can be challenging. Having as few transitions as possible is important. An environmentally based program can accomplish this because you are not constantly moving toddlers from one planned activity to another throughout the day. Of course, eliminating all transitions is impossible. Children need to transition into your program, and once there, there are transitions to meal times, outdoor play, naps, and so on. Here are some tips to make transitions easier on you and the toddlers in your care.

- ✿ Plan ahead: Make transitions short and sweet. Know ahead of time what you plan to do with the children each day, and have a rough idea of when. Make sure all caregivers have a specific task to help move the children smoothly to the new activity (for example, assist with coats, hold the door, monitor children in the next space, and so on).

- ✿ Be organized: Arrange your environment to facilitate easy transitions. If you are taking children outside, keep everything you need (phone, emergency numbers, and so on) in one convenient place. Make it easy for children to get any materials they may need, such as coats before heading outside or soap, water, and a towel before snack. Organizing and labeling items makes it easier to find what you need quickly. Do whatever you can to shorten the time children spend waiting for you.

- ✿ Give warnings: Let children know ahead of time that they will soon have to stop what they are doing. Give them a few minutes' warning, enough time to finish their activities.

You may even want to consider several warnings: one at five minutes, one at three minutes, and one at one minute. Time is still a concept beyond the grasp of most toddlers, so make the warnings concrete and consistent. Use visual cues, such as a timer that children can see. Play or sing a song; when the song ends, it is time for children to stop what they are doing and clean up. Make sure you use the same song each time.

✿ Divide into smaller groups: Smaller groups can be more manageable. Have children engaged in a fun activity or free play, and invite a few children at a time to move on to the next event of the day. This works especially well when space is limited, such as in the bathroom washing hands before lunch.

✿ Guide children through song and action: Rituals work beautifully to guide children through transitions by bringing structure to an unstructured time. Sing a song at clean-up time that reminds children of what they should do to help clean up. Have a welcome and goodbye routine that might include a song, a hug, and specific actions for putting away or taking out personal belongings. Play follow the leader to move children from space to space (indoors to outdoors, to lunch, and so on).

## Evaluating

At the end of the day, evaluate. Talk with other program staff. Did you do the special activities you had planned? Did you meet any goals or objectives? If not, why not? Maybe the activities, or even the goals themselves, were inappropriate, or perhaps something unexpected happened. Could you do anything differently next time to make the experience better? If things went even better than expected, try to identify why. Do not limit your evaluations to the special activities that you plan. Toddlers grow and change quickly. A good toddler program should constantly be evaluating the following:

✿ Changes to the environment

✿ Changes to the daily routine

✿ Program goals and objectives

✿ Individual child goals and objectives

✿ Family involvement

✿ Special activities

Even toddler behavior can help you to evaluate your program. Much of the "bad" behavior young children exhibit can be avoided by making changes to their environment. If you are having behavior problems in your toddler group, evaluate the following:

✿ Expectations: Are they realistic?

✿ Materials: Are there too few or too many? Do not expect toddlers to share; they are not developmentally ready!

✿ Children's experiences: Are the children bored, frustrated, or overwhelmed?

✿ Space: Is it too crowded or too open? Bad behaviors such as hitting or biting are often a result of toddlers not having enough space, while constant running might mean that your space is too open.

✿ Scheduling: Are children required to wait or sit still too much? Is the schedule chaotic or unpredictable? Is it incompatible with the toddlers' internal schedules?

✿ Temptations: Are forbidden areas or materials too easy to get to?

✿ Noise: Is the environment too noisy or overstimulating?


On the next page is a form to help you plan and evaluate your program.

# Weekly Planning Form

Week of_____

Experiences and skills to emphasize_____

| Changes to the environment |
|---|
|  |

Special activities to offer this week

|  | Monday | Tuesday | Wednesday | Thursday | Friday |
|---|---|---|---|---|---|
| Songs Stories Games |  |  |  |  |  |
| Indoor Exploration |  |  |  |  |  |
| Outdoor Exploration |  |  |  |  |  |

| Changes to daily routines |
|---|
|  |

| Involving families |
|---|
|  |

| My to-do list |
|---|
|  |

# Chapter 4: Assessment

You have gotten your program up and running. Your environment and schedule have been carefully thought out, and you have taken the time to select experiential activities for your group of toddlers. But how do you know if you are being effective?

It is time to think about how to evaluate each child's progress. Assessments are the final component to a successful program. By documenting the toddlers' progress in an organized and consistent way, you will not only learn about where each child is developmentally throughout the year, you will also gain valuable information about how successfully your program is meeting the needs of the children in your care. Armed with this information, you can modify the activities, curriculum, or physical environment to grow and improve your overall program.

## Authentic Assessment Practices

A multiple-choice exam taken on a particular day often does not show a person's true knowledge or abilities. Young children are even more sensitive to pressure or "forced" situations. Often, toddlers will not perform for you at all. To get a clear picture of a child's abilities, your assessment should include the following aspects:

- ⊡ Be used in a child's natural play environment: Children are more likely to experiment with emerging skills when they are in comfortable, familiar situations. A natural play environment will give you a more accurate measure of the skills a child is working on.

- ⊡ Be closely related to your daily program or curriculum: Bringing in an assessment tool that is very different from what children are used to doing in your program can be unsettling to children, and so you are unlikely to get an accurate measure of their abilities.

- ☢ Measure developmentally appropriate skills: Be sure the guidelines you are using are developmentally appropriate for the ages you are working with (do not place preschool expectations on toddlers), and be sure that any activities you use to test skills are also appropriate for each child's stage of development.

- ☢ Cover all relevant domains, and account for different learning styles: Remember, children develop holistically, meaning that as their motor skills develop, so do their language skills. As their language skills develop, so do their social skills, and so forth. While we may think of each area as developing individually, all areas are actually quite interconnected. Be sure you include a variety of activities in your evaluation of a child to ensure you are measuring progress in all areas of development and are allowing for those with different learning styles to excel.

- ☢ Be ongoing: To truly get a handle a child's progress, assessments should be done several times throughout the year. As you look back over previous assessments, evidence of a child's growth (or lack of growth) will be clear.

- ☢ Include the family as an important source of information: Families are partners in their children's education. The more information you can get about a child's cultural background, home life, and behaviors at home, the more complete a picture you will have of that child, and then you can interpret assessment results more accurately.

## Some Assessment Options

The more methods you use to measure a child's progress, the more accurate a picture you will get. Of course, you want any method you use to be in line with the authentic assessment practices mentioned above. Two methods that work especially well with young children are the individual portfolio and planned activity assessments using an assessment instrument (rubric or chart).

### The Individual Portfolio

An individual portfolio is a three-ring binder or file in which you keep samples of a child's work that you collect regularly throughout the year. This has the advantage of working seamlessly with your everyday curriculum and activities. Portfolios give you a lot of flexibility regarding how you present evidence of a child's progress, and they present a clear picture of how a child progresses over time.

You can use photos, observations and anecdotal records, samples of a child's work, notes from family members, videos, and so on as entries in a portfolio. Be sure to include typical work at different points in the year as well as important "firsts" for each child (for example, the first time she uses a word to communicate or the first time she climbs into the loft). With so many possibilities, creating a good portfolio can feel overwhelming. Here are some tips to keep you organized and focused.

- For each child, use a three-ring binder containing clear sleeves for storing work. Label each binder with the child's name.

- Use dividers to create distinct assessment areas that make sense for your program. For example, motor, language, social and emotional, cognitive, and so on. It is inevitable that some of the evidence you collect will fit into more than one category. This is why it is important that you think about the reason you are choosing to include each portfolio entry.

- Plan in advance. Think about what skills you want to track, the "firsts" you want to collect, and how you want to show evidence of progress. Make the decision to gather specific work samples or other evidence at specific points in the year. This does not mean that on the first Tuesday in October, you will take a fingerpainting sample from everyone. You want to make sure that the samples you select represent what is typical for that child. If he is having unusual difficulty that day or is showing a lack of interest, wait until you have a more typical sample to enter.

- Use your state's standards, your program's curriculum guidelines, or the developmental milestones included in this book to guide your planning. This way, your program will be able to show clear evidence of working toward those goals.

- Document the reasons for including each entry. Use the forms provided in this book, or create your own method for explaining each entry. Just be sure that each is dated and includes an explanation of what skill it is intended to showcase.

- Be selective about the work you choose to include. Each entry should show a child's progress in the developmental area, skill set, or learning standard that you are tracking (for example, a drawing sample taken at the beginning of the year, the first time a child creates a circle or enclosed form, another drawing sample taken later in the year). But also include individualized items that showcase a child's unique skills or interests, such as photos, taken over time, of rows of blocks the child enjoys forming.

Use the following form to describe each portfolio piece you collect. Simply fasten it to the work collected or slide it into a clear sheet protector along with the work sample. As you look back over the portfolio, these forms will help you to identify the purpose of each piece in the collection.

**Portfolio Piece**

Child's Name: _Parker_      Date: _1/17/11_

Activity: _Roller Painting_      Collected by: _Susan_

Skill(s) displayed:
Rotates wrist to manipulate objects

Comments:
Parker worked hard to get the ball to move all over the paper

## Planned Activity Assessments

During planned activity assessments, teachers use an assessment instrument, such as a chart or rubric, to track evidence of the skills a child demonstrates during that particular planned activity. Children participate in the planned activity as they usually would in a regular classroom activity. The only difference is that teachers stand by to observe and record the skills they see the children demonstrate in their normal course of play or exploration. The choice of activity and recording chart are carefully planned in advance. Activities and observations typically go on over a period of time, usually several weeks, to ensure that each child is assessed while exhibiting typical behavior. Again, you do not want to evaluate a child when she is having a bad day. Activity assessments are then repeated later in the year. Planned activity assessments allow teachers to clearly see the skills that each child in their program demonstrates at a particular point in time. This type of assessment is a great way to get a baseline measure of a child's skills, and when repeated again later in the year, evidence of progress (or lack of progress) is very clear.

While it may seem much simpler than maintaining individual portfolios, planned activity assessments require a lot of thought and staff time. Here are some tips to make them successful.

- Plan to complete assessments on all children at least twice a year to show progress. To ensure that all children are comfortable in your program before being assessed, wait at least six weeks after the first day before doing an initial assessment.

- Make sure assessed activities are natural play situations for the children. This ensures that the children are comfortable demonstrating their true skills.

- Be clear about the skills you are looking for, and prepare a recording chart in advance. An example of a recording chart is included in this book.

- Select a few high-interest activities that lend themselves to assessing a variety of skills. You want to be sure the activities you choose will engage a variety of children who have different interests, skills, and learning styles. Many of the activities in this book make great planned assessment activities.

- Set up several planned activity stations with a staff person assigned to each. Be sure you have enough staff or additional adult support on hand to encourage children who are not engaged in the targeted activities to become involved, or else make sure these children are adequately supervised.

- Allow plenty of time, up to six weeks, to complete assessments on all children. The first assessment period always takes the longest. Once caregivers become familiar with the children, the assessment procedure, and the activities, future assessments will go much more smoothly.

- After the assessment is over, be prepared to shadow those children who you feel did not show their true skills. Make notes of the skills you see in their everyday play. You want to be sure you get an accurate read on every child's abilities.

## Assessment Instrument
### 12 to 24 months

Activity: Visiting Vehicles
modification: used ball instead of car

Child's Name: Claudia

Observer: Erin

**Key:**
2- skill mastery
1- skill emerging
0- Not showing interest yet

Dates of Assessments
10/11

| | Milestone/Standard | Notes | 10/11 | | | |
|---|---|---|---|---|---|---|
| **Social/ Emotional** | Expresses individuality- may insist on doing things, says "no" frequently | | not observed | | | |
| | Expresses strong feelings and frustration | | not observed | | | |
| | Seeks approval of parents/caregivers, may be clingy | 10/11- looked to me after each roll | 1 | | | |
| | Enjoys the company of peers | 10/11- laughed with others | 2 | | | |
| | Models adult behavior | | 1 | | | |
| | Identifies one or more body parts | | n/o | | | |
| | Sensitive to the reactions of others | 10/11 - visibly upset when Alice threw the ball | 1 | | | |
| | Able to follow clear, simple rules | | 2 | | | |
| | Begins to control feelings and use words to express them | | 1 | | | |
| | Showing awareness of the feelings of others | | 1 | | | |
| | Begins using names for self and others | | 1 | | | |
| | | | | | | |
| | | | | | | |

Use this form to help you identify the skills children demonstrate while you observe an assessment activity. Note any modifications you make. By using one form per child and by using the same form again later in the year, evidence of progress and development will be very clear.

## The Family Component

Families are the best source of information about the children in your care. Be sure to include them in the assessment process. At the beginning of each school year, encourage families to fill out a simple form that will help you get to know their children's needs, personalities, likes, and interests. You will also want to learn about the families' routines, goals, and concerns regarding their children. We have included a sample form in this book. You may want to invite family members to fill it out during an initial home visit, or include it among the required paperwork for enrollment into your program. Either way, it will send a clear message to family members that you view them as playing an important role in your program and that their voices will be heard.

Continue to keep the lines of communication with families open throughout the year. Many children behave quite differently at school than they do at home, so the picture of a child's developmental progress may be incomplete without some idea of the skills he may be demonstrating at home. One way to consistently communicate with family members is to pass a journal back and forth from home to school. This weekly informal correspondence allows teachers and family members to share anecdotes about the children along with information about how the children are spending their time in your program and at home. It is also a great way for families and teachers to share any questions or concerns. Of course, sensitive issues should be addressed face-to-face and not in a journal. Specific journal entries can be used as anecdotal evidence of progress in a portfolio.

Regular family member–teacher conferences are another great way to keep the lines of communication open. These can take place at your program or at the child's home. When you are scheduling conferences, make an effort to accommodate a variety of family work schedules. Be flexible and offer choices. Because these meetings are private and face-to-face, they provide a great opportunity to share your concerns about a child, and they give families a chance to bring up their own issues or to ask you questions. While a family member–teacher conference does not have to be formal, it is important that you come prepared with specific information about each child's progress. Take notes at these meetings, and review your notes with families before the meetings are over to make sure you have accurately described their questions, issues, or concerns. Simple informal conversations at pickup and drop-off times are also a wonderful way to promote communication with family members, though these quick conversations are more difficult to document.

Finally, once you have completed your assessments (or periodically throughout the year, if you are using individual portfolios), take the time to talk with families about the information you have collected about their children. Share with families the information you have gathered through the assessments, and give families an idea of how their children are doing on a day-to-day basis. Listen to the family members, including their reactions to the assessment information. Because some children display skills at home that they do not exhibit in a group care setting, families need the opportunity to share their observations and information with you. Also, many developmental or health issues are first noticed when toddlers do not follow the typical path through developmental milestones, and this information should be shared with families. The best forum for such a review is a family member–teacher conference as described above.

## Creating an Assessment Plan

Planning is the most important piece of an assessment. Take the time to think about your program (staff availability, state mandates, program goals) and what it is that you are trying to learn or gain by doing assessments. This information will help you to choose the type of assessment method or methods that best meet your needs.

Once you know why and how you are doing assessments, it is time to select the activities that will best give children the opportunity to demonstrate the skills you are monitoring. The final planning step is to map out your time frame and consider the logistics (staff requirements, materials, space) to get it done.

| Steps for Successful Assessments |
| --- |
| 1. Identify why you are doing assessments or assessment goals (to monitor progress, evaluate a program, or comply with mandates). |
| 2. Identify assessment methods that will achieve these goals. |
| 3. Select curriculum-based activities that will showcase targeted skills. |
| 4. Plan the time frame and logistics. |
| 5. Collect the data. |
| 6. Evaluate the data. |

A good assessment activity is one that gives children with different learning styles and temperaments the opportunity to demonstrate a variety of skills. Many of the activities you typically do in your program every day are great assessment opportunities. Integrating your assessments into your regular program routine is most comfortable for children and will give you a more accurate read on their skills and abilities.

| Great Assessment Opportunities (and Some Developmental Areas They Showcase) |
| --- |
| ✿ Classroom routines and transitions (social and emotional, listening) |
| ✿ Meals and snack (social and emotional, language, motor) |
| ✿ Songs, fingerplays, and story time (language, listening, motor) |
| ✿ Outdoor play (motor, social and emotional, language, cognitive) |
| ✿ Dramatic play (language, motor, social and emotional, cognitive) |
| ✿ Art experiences and manipulatives (motor, cognitive, language) |
| ✿ Conversations with familiar adults (language, listening, social and emotional, cognitive) |

## Using the Results

Of course, you want to be sure that you track the progress of individual children as their development is monitored and evaluated throughout the year. This information is useful to help caregivers plan new activities and experiences that will support a toddler's development. Sharing this information with families is also beneficial. It allows families to see the value of your program and helps them to get a clear picture of their child's growth and progress.

But the usefulness of these data goes beyond monitoring individual children. Once you have compiled all of that data, take the time to look at the big picture. In addition to informing you about the progress of individual children, your assessment data can provide useful information about your program. Look at the overall skill development of all of the children in each of the different domains or learning areas. This will give you an idea of how well your program is meeting your state's guidelines or your program goals. Is there an area in which children are not progressing consistently? Do you notice any common traits among the children who are progressing more slowly? Are the children of the same temperament, cultural background, or stage of development? This information could give you valuable insight into your program's strengths and weaknesses. Use it to help you to make decisions about professional development, teaching, and curriculum. When data on individuals are compiled together to create a picture of your entire program, authentic assessments can help improve overall program quality.

## Sample Basic Assessment Schedule

Month 1
- ✿ Send out family questionnaire or conduct home visits
- ✿ Plan assessment goals, select initial assessment activities, and prepare forms
- ✿ Create a portfolio binder for each child

Month 2
- ✿ Review family questionnaires with staff
- ✿ Plan and coordinate teacher schedules to perform initial assessments
- ✿ Begin collecting portfolio pieces

Month 3
- ✿ Perform initial planned activity assessments
- ✿ Continue collecting portfolio pieces

Month 4
- ✿ Schedule family member–teacher conferences to review initial planned activity assessment results and individual portfolios
- ✿ Continue collecting portfolio pieces

Month 5
- ✿ Plan and coordinate teacher schedules for midyear planned activity assessments using the same activities and forms as the initial assessments
- ✿ Continue collecting portfolio pieces

Month 6
- ✿ Perform planned activity assessments
- ✿ Continue collecting portfolio pieces

Month 7
- ✿ Schedule family member conferences to review planned activity assessments and individual portfolios
- ✿ Continue collecting portfolio pieces

Month 8
- ✿ Continue collecting portfolio pieces

Month 9
- ✿ Plan and coordinate teacher schedules for end-of-year planned activity assessments using the same activities and forms as the initial assessments
- ✿ Continue collecting portfolio pieces

Month 10
- ✿ Perform planned activity assessments
- ✿ Continue collecting portfolio pieces

Month 11
- ✿ Schedule family member conferences to review initial planned activity assessment results and individual portfolios
- ✿ Continue collecting portfolio pieces

Month 12
- ✿ As a staff, review all assessment results and portfolios to assess your overall program quality. Make plans for program improvements and adjustments

## About Me and My Family

Date: _____

Child's Name: _____

Date of Birth: _____

*A note to family members: This form will help us get to know your child and your family. Knowing your child's regular routines, likes and dislikes, and your goals for your child will help us to better serve your whole family.*

### About Me

**My personality in general is**_____

**I was born**  ❑ Full-term  ❑ Preterm

**When I get sick, it is often because of or accompanied by (please check all that apply):**

❑ Ear Infections  ❑ RSV  ❑ Stomachache  ❑ Diarrhea
❑ Seizures  ❑ Asthma  ❑ Urinary Infection  ❑ Headaches  ❑ Cough

**When it is time to eat, I like to use (please check all that apply):**

❑ A bottle  ❑ My hands  ❑ A spoon  ❑ A fork  ❑ I like to be fed  ❑ I eat on my own

**In general, I like** ❑ Most foods  ❑ Some foods  ❑ I'm a picky eater

**My potty words are** _____(urination) and _____(bowel movement).

**Where I Live** *(list residences and typical days at each home)*

| Whose House | Address | Days of the Week |
|---|---|---|

1 _____

_____

2 _____

_____

3 _____

_____

**Who Lives with Me** *(list names and relationship to child, ages of other children, and do not forget pets!)*

House 1: _____

House 2: _____

House 3: _____

**On a normal day at home, I...***(House 1)*
(describe daily routine in detail) _____

_____

_____

_____

**On a normal day at home, I...***(House 2)*
(describe daily routine in detail) _____

_____

_____

_____

**On a normal day at home, I...***(House 3)*
(describe daily routine in detail) _____

_____

_____

_____

**My family is excited for me to learn and grow.**

A few things they hope I will do this year are _____

_____

_____

A few things I hope I will do this year are _____

_____

_____

**Growing up can be hard.**

A few things my family is worried about are _____

_____

_____

A few things I'm worried about are _____

_____

_____

A few things I love are_____

_____

_____

A few things I do not like at all are_____

_____

_____

Thank you for taking the time to fill out this form! It will help us to get to know your child and your family.

## Assessment Instrument

12–18 months

Activity:

Child's Name: _____

Observer:_____

**Key:**

3 = Skill Mastery: Demonstrates correctly 90% or more of the time

2 = Skill Practicing: Demonstrates correctly 50% of the time

1 = Skill Emerging: Demonstrates correctly less than 50% of the time

0 = Not showing interest yet

| | Milestone or Standard | Notes | Date | Date | Date |
|---|---|---|---|---|---|
| **Social and Emotional** | Expresses individuality: may insist on doing things, says no frequently | | | | |
| | Expresses strong feelings and frustration | | | | |
| | Seeks approval of family members and caregivers, may be clingy | | | | |
| | Enjoys the company of peers | | | | |
| | Models adult behavior | | | | |
| | Able to follow clear, simple rules | | | | |
| | Sensitive to the reactions of others | | | | |
| | | | | | |
| | | | | | |
| **Gross Motor** | Walks independently | | | | |
| | Pulls, pushes, and carries items | | | | |
| | Squats | | | | |
| | Walks backward | | | | |
| | Climbs larger furniture | | | | |
| | | | | | |
| | | | | | |

| Milestone or Standard | Notes | Date | Date | Date |
|---|---|---|---|---|
| **Fine Motor** | | | | |
| Turns pages in a books | | | | |
| Feeds self with spoon | | | | |
| Uses a cup | | | | |
| Stacks objects | | | | |
| | | | | |
| | | | | |
| **Language** | | | | |
| Says 5–10 words relatively clearly | | | | |
| Directs the attention of others | | | | |
| Asks for things by pointing | | | | |
| Points to objects when asked | | | | |
| Follows simple commands | | | | |
| Looks at person speaking | | | | |
| | | | | |
| | | | | |

**Assessment Instrument**

18–24 months

Activity:

Child's Name: _____

Observer:_____

**Key:**

3 = Skill Mastery: Demonstrates correctly 90% or more of the time

2 = Skill Practicing: Demonstrates correctly 50% of the time

1 = Skill Emerging: Demonstrates correctly less than 50% of the time

0 = Not showing interest yet

| | Milestone or Standard | Notes | Date | Date | Date |
|---|---|---|---|---|---|
| Social and Emotional | Expresses strong feelings and frustration | | | | |
| | Seeks approval of family members and caregivers, may be clingy | | | | |
| | Models adult behavior | | | | |
| | Enjoys being near other children | | | | |
| | Uses the imagination in play (making sounds for a car, and so on) | | | | |
| | | | | | |
| | | | | | |
| Gross Motor | Runs | | | | |
| | Walks down stairs | | | | |
| | Throws a ball | | | | |
| | | | | | |
| | | | | | |
| Fine Motor | Uses a cup | | | | |
| | Opens and closes doors, drawers, containers, and so on | | | | |
| | Removes clothing | | | | |
| | | | | | |
| | | | | | |

ASSESSMENT

| Milestone or Standard | Notes | Date | Date | Date |
|---|---|---|---|---|
| Able to identify some body parts | | | | |
| Puts two words together to make simple sentences | | | | |
| Uses 1- to 2-word questions | | | | |
| Follows simple commands | | | | |
| Points to objects when asked | | | | |
| | | | | |
| | | | | |

Language

## Assessment Instrument

24–30 months

Activity:

Child's Name: _____

Observer:_____

**Key:**

3 = Skill Mastery: Demonstrates correctly 90% or more of the time

2 = Skill Practicing: Demonstrates correctly 50% of the time

1 = Skill Emerging: Demonstrates correctly less than 50% of the time

0 = Not showing interest yet

| | Milestone or Standard | Notes | Date | Date | Date |
|---|---|---|---|---|---|
| **Social and Emotional** | Tests limits | | | | |
| | Sensitive to the reactions of others | | | | |
| | Follows clear, simple rules | | | | |
| | Uses name of self and others | | | | |
| | | | | | |
| | | | | | |
| **Gross Motor** | Jumps with both feet | | | | |
| | Walks backward | | | | |
| | | | | | |
| | | | | | |
| **Fine Motor** | Draws a line | | | | |
| | Beginning to put on clothes | | | | |
| | Unties and unzips | | | | |
| | | | | | |
| | | | | | |

| | Milestone or Standard | Notes | Date | Date | Date |
|---|---|---|---|---|---|
| Language | Uses pronouns (*I*, *me*, *you*, and so on) | | | | |
| | Sings songs | | | | |
| | Speech is understandable more than half of the time | | | | |
| | Follows two commands (get the book and put it in the basket) | | | | |
| | | | | | |
| | | | | | |

## Assessment Instrument

30–36 months

Activity:

Child's Name: _____

Observer: _____

**Key:**

3 = Skill Mastery: Demonstrates correctly 90% or more of the time

2 = Skill Practicing: Demonstrates correctly 50% of the time

1 = Skill Emerging: Demonstrates correctly less than 50% of the time

0 = Not showing interest yet

| | Milestone or Standard | Notes | Date | Date | Date |
|---|---|---|---|---|---|
| **Social and Emotional** | Developing self-control | | | | |
| | Beginning to use words to express feelings | | | | |
| | Demonstrating awareness of the feelings of others | | | | |
| | Plays with others | | | | |
| | Engages in more complex imaginative play (acting as a character or creating a story) | | | | |
| | Expresses interest in toileting | | | | |
| | | | | | |
| | | | | | |
| **Gross Motor** | Kicks a ball | | | | |
| | Stands on one foot | | | | |
| | Stands or walks on tiptoes | | | | |
| | Beginning to climb stairs by alternating feet | | | | |
| | | | | | |
| | | | | | |

| | Milestone or Standard | Notes | Date | Date | Date |
|---|---|---|---|---|---|
| **Fine Motor** | Threads large beads | | | | |
| | Learning to use scissors | | | | |
| | Pours liquids into cups or bowls | | | | |
| | | | | | |
| **Language** | Speech is understandable most of the time | | | | |
| | Has words for most things and familiar people | | | | |
| | Beginning to acquire grammar | | | | |
| | Recounts events of the day | | | | |
| | Understands more abstract words such as *big*, *little*, *in*, and *on* | | | | |
| | | | | | |
| | | | | | |

**Assessment Instrument**

Activity:

Child's Name: _____

Observer: _____

Child's Age: _____

Key:

3 = Skill Mastery: Demonstrates correctly 90% or more of the time

2 = Skill Practicing: Demonstrates correctly 50% of the time

1 = Skill Emerging: Demonstrates correctly less than 50% of the time

0 = Not showing interest yet

| Development Area | Milestone or Standard | Notes | Date | Date | Date |
|---|---|---|---|---|---|
| | | | | | |
| | | | | | |
| | | | | | |
| | | | | | |
| | | | | | |
| | | | | | |
| | | | | | |
| | | | | | |
| | | | | | |
| | | | | | |
| | | | | | |
| | | | | | |
| | | | | | |
| | | | | | |

## Portfolio Piece

Child's Name: _____     Date: _____

Activity: _____     Collected by: _____

Skill(s) displayed:

Comments:

## Portfolio Piece

Child's Name: _____     Date: _____

Activity: _____     Collected by: _____

Skill(s) displayed:

Comments:

## Portfolio Piece

Child's Name: _____     Date: _____

Activity: _____     Collected by: _____

Skill(s) displayed:

Comments:

# Chapter 5:
# Child Growth
# and Development

**Toddlers are developing at an incredible rate. It seems as if every day, they make new discoveries and learn to do something new. From the day they are born, young children are developing motor skills, learning to communicate and interact with the adults in their lives, experiencing and learning to express their emotions, and developing their senses to explore the world. These areas of development are all interconnected; growth in one area will encourage the development of another area. As a toddler learns to pull a lever on a toy (motor skill), he sees a door pop open or hears a sound or feels a vibration (sensory). He may respond with a verbal outburst. He may say, "Uh-oh!" or "Moo!" if a cow appears, developing his language skills. As the toddler's brain processes and organizes these experiences, he is beginning to understand cause and effect, and all of these experiences are laying the foundation for future learning.**

Developmental milestones are important tools for caregivers. Understanding what skills children generally have at a specific age can help you to know what to expect from the children in your care. It can also help you identify children who are not developing as expected. But never forget that these milestones are only a guideline. They represent the average age. The actual age that a child will reach a milestone varies greatly from child to child. What is less likely to vary is the order in which children move through the milestones. Skipping milestones altogether or persistent and long delays in reaching milestones could be signs that a child could benefit from the insight of a specialist.

We know every child is different. What we need to remember is that every child will develop at his own pace. Do not rush children. Toddlers want and need to perfect each new skill that they discover. For example, resist the temptation to carry a child down the stairs or to put him into his chair because it is faster. Instead be patient, and fill their days with opportunities to practice developing skills.

Here are brief descriptions of developmental skills typical of toddlers (12–36 months), as well as milestone charts divided into the development areas of fine motor, gross motor, language, and social and emotional skills.

# Developmental Milestones by Age

## 12 to 18 months

These children are constantly moving about and are familiar with household objects. They are learning to open drawers and doors and to manipulate objects. Many toddlers at this age use two-word sentences and can verbally communicate wants but still rely heavily on gestures. They are learning to use a spoon independently and to drink from a cup but may spill fluids out the

sides. Gross motor skills include crawling backward, walking, beginning to run, climbing stairs and chairs, throwing objects indiscriminately, and learning to help put on and take off clothes. These new skills require that they be watched closely. Children at this age like to help others and imitate adults. They are becoming more independent and separate more easily from their family members or caregivers. They may take only one nap some days but need time to slowly reorient after waking.

## 18 to 24 months

At this age, toddlers are very curious about everything and are much more interested in satisfying this curiosity than in following rules or being safe. They may know up to 50 words and may mimic adult speech. As their vocabulary grows, they enjoy talking about pictures, books, and their own actions. They also like to explore rhythm and rhyme in language and are more aware of colors. Their bodies have grown and a larger lung capacity may spark a new enthusiasm for yelling. At the table, they show strong food preferences and can feed themselves pretty well using a cup and spoon, although they may spill on occasion. They enjoy opening and closing doors and drawers and manipulating anything with a handle, lever, or button that they come across. Gross motor skills include sitting in a variety of positions, kicking or chasing a ball, running, and improved balance. They can wash their hands and are learning to balance blocks on top of one another. They may be able to undress but will have a hard time with buttons, zippers, and so on. These toddlers are very egocentric and have difficulty sharing, but they respond well to positive reinforcement and praise. At this age, a child's temperament is well defined, and it is not uncommon for toddlers of all temperaments to throw tantrums to get their way. These children need a one- to two-hour nap.

## 24 to 30 months

At this age, the toddler brain is becoming more sophisticated. Curiosity continues to drive children's explorations, and their intellectual development enables them to begin to understand somewhat abstract concepts such as "one" and sorting or matching objects by color, form, and size. These toddlers enjoy simple puzzles and block building. Their language skills have increased greatly. They can speak three- to five-word sentences with a definite intent to communicate and are beginning to use pronouns. They understand most of what is said and often ask questions. Their fine motor skills are much improved, enabling them to make lines with a crayon and to untie and unzip. Gross motor skills include jumping, beginning to ride a tricycle, walking up and down stairs, and beginning to self-dress with help. At this age, toddlers' emotions often shift between extremes. They want to be in control and are easily frustrated. They are more easily overwhelmed by their emotions when tired. These toddlers continue to need a nap but may begin to protest against taking one.

## 30 to 36 months

These older toddlers have a greatly increased vocabulary and are beginning to acquire grammar, although they still make mistakes. They are also able to understand more abstract concepts such as *big* and *little* or *in* and *on* and are beginning to express their feelings with words. Their fine motor skills continue to develop and may include threading large beads, using scissors, and pouring liquids into containers. Gross motor skills have also improved, and these children can stand on one foot, walk on tiptoes, and perhaps climb stairs putting only one foot on each step. Older toddlers are emotionally complicated and often test limits. They

CHILD GROWTH AND DEVELOPMENT

tend to go back and forth between acting like a baby and acting like a "big kid," and they expect you to respond quite differently to them depending on their mood. Socially, they are becoming more aware of others and enjoy playing alongside and possibly with other children. Their self-control is also improving, especially when they are given clear, simple rules. Naps are still important.

# Milestones by Area of Development

## Social and Emotional Milestones

| Age | Skills |
|-----|--------|
| 12–18 months | ✿ Begins to develop self-image<br>✿ Expresses individuality—may insist on doing things, may say "no" or tell you what to do<br>✿ Sensitive to the reactions of others<br>✿ Enjoys being with other children but cannot yet share<br>✿ Able to follow clear, simple rules |
| 18–24 months | ✿ Expresses strong feelings and frustration<br>✿ May have occasional tantrums<br>✿ Enjoys being near other children but plays independently<br>✿ Uses the imagination in play (for example, making sounds for a car) |
| 24–30 months | ✿ Sensitive to reactions of others, very aware of your tone and words—this shapes self-image<br>✿ Tests limits<br>✿ Can follow clear, simple rules<br>✿ Uses name of self and others |
| 30–36 months | ✿ Emotions shift between extremes<br>✿ Begins to develop self-control<br>✿ May use words to express feelings<br>✿ Becoming aware of the feelings of others<br>✿ Enjoys playing with others<br>✿ Frequently engages in more complex imaginative play, acting as a character or creating a story<br>✿ May show an interest in toileting |

## Gross Motor Milestones

| Age | Gross Motor Skills |
|-----|--------------------|
| 12-18 months | ✿ Walks independently<br>✿ Pulls, pushes, and carries items<br>✿ Squats<br>✿ Walks backward<br>✿ Climbs larger furniture |
| 18-24 months | ✿ Runs<br>✿ Walks down stairs<br>✿ Throws a ball |
| 24-30 months | ✿ Jumps with both feet<br>✿ Walks backward |
| 30-36 months | ✿ Kicks a ball<br>✿ Stands on one foot<br>✿ Stands and walks on tiptoes<br>✿ May be able to climb stairs putting one foot on each step |

## Fine Motor Milestones

| Age | Fine Motor Skills |
|-----|-------------------|
| 12-18 months | ✿ Turns pages in a book<br>✿ Holds a crayon<br>✿ Feeds self with a spoon<br>✿ Stacks objects |
| 18-24 months | ✿ Uses a cup independently<br>✿ Opens and closes doors, drawers, containers, and so on<br>✿ Removes clothing |
| 24-30 months | ✿ Draws a line<br>✿ Beginning to put on clothes<br>✿ Unties and unzips |
| 30-36 months | ✿ Threads large beads<br>✿ Learning to use scissors<br>✿ Pours liquids into cups or bowls |

## Language Milestones

| Age | Talking | Listening |
| --- | --- | --- |
| 12–18 months | ✿ Says 5–10 words relatively clearly<br>✿ Directs the attention of others toward things of interest<br>✿ Asks for things by pointing | ✿ Looks at person speaking<br>✿ Follows simple commands<br>✿ Points to objects when asked (body parts, pictures of familiar objects in a book) |
| 18–24 months | ✿ Able to identify some body parts<br>✿ Puts two words together to make simple sentences: "more juice"<br>✿ Uses 1- to 2-word questions, "go bye-bye?" | ✿ Enjoys hearing rhythm and rhyme in language |
| 24–30 months | ✿ Uses pronouns (*I*, *me*, *you*, and so on)<br>✿ Sings songs<br>✿ Speech is understandable more than half the time | ✿ Follows two commands: "get the book, *and* put it in the basket" |
| 30–36 months | ✿ Speech is understandable most of the time<br>✿ Has words for most everything<br>✿ Beginning to acquire grammar, but makes many mistakes<br>✿ Recounts events of the day | ✿ Understands more abstract concept words: *big*, *little*, *in*, and *on* |

# Working with Young Children with Special Needs

While every child is unique and develops differently, some toddlers may enter your program with clearly identified special needs. But many children with special needs are identified in the toddler years by their caregivers. No matter how or when a child is identified as having a special need, it is clear that early intervention and the support of specialists greatly benefit these children and their families.

## Understanding the Language of Special Needs

Because it is likely that you will provide care for a toddler with an identified or unidentified special need, it is important that you become familiar with some of the language and terms used in the field of special education:

**At-Risk:** a term used to describe a child who, because of environmental, socioeconomic, family history, or other factors, is considered more likely to develop a temporary or permanent special need. For example, a child with normal hearing who has parents who have hearing difficulties may be exposed to less spoken language than other children of the same age. Because of this, the child would be at risk for developing a language delay.

**Developmental Delay:** a term used when a child's development in one or more areas is not progressing at a typical rate, even when keeping in mind the great variety of rates at which children develop. For example, a 20-month-old who is not yet walking may be considered to have a motor delay. Sometimes doctors will describe a child as having a developmental delay when they have identified a concern in a child's developmental progress but are waiting to see if the child will eventually "catch up" to his peers in terms of development. If the child does not seem to be progressing, a more specific diagnosis may later be explored. Developmental delays are often seen in the following areas:

- Cognitive
- Motor
- Sensory (including vision and hearing)
- Communication/Language
- Social/Emotional
- Adaptive (self-help)

**Early Intervention:** a term that describes services provided by specialists to infants and toddlers (birth to 36 months) with special needs, with the goal of supporting their development in an area or areas of need.

## Important Information about Special Education Law

The federal government has strong laws in place to protect and support individuals with special needs. The Individuals with Disabilities Act of 2004 ensures special education services to all eligible children, including infants and toddlers. It also governs how states and public agencies provide early intervention and other services and includes a federal grant program that provides funding to assist those organizations providing these services. Individual states decide whether they will provide services only to those with a diagnosed disability or developmental delay or if they will also provide services to children with at-risk conditions. States also must designate a lead agency to manage referrals and determine eligibility and are required to provide a toll-free phone number to assist providers and families through the referral process. If you have questions about this process or eligibility requirements in your state, contact your state's designated lead agency. A quick online search or call to a local pediatrician's office should get you the toll-free phone number and agency name.

## Observing Toddlers

Observant caregivers play an important role in the early identification of special needs. The attention and care you give each toddler enable you to really get to know an individual child's strengths and weaknesses, likes and dislikes. It is likely you also have a lot of experience with many different children of the same age. Your knowledge of typical development in toddlers (keeping in mind the great variety of ages at which typical children achieve developmental milestones), combined with your experience, may put you in a position to notice a child whose development does not seem to be following the typical path. This is often referred to as "atypical development."

Despite your desire to do what is best for the child and your strong belief that there may be an issue that needs to be explored, sharing your concern with parents is daunting. It is helpful to have already built strong relationships with families when you do decide to share your

concerns. When the child you are concerned about is not well supported at home or has an inconsistent or even volatile home life, the family member–caregiver relationship is often challenging, but in these situations, a positive relationship with the family is especially important and deserves extra effort. Relationships with families grow when you communicate regularly and openly, sharing positive moments as much as possible and being honest about issues that arise. Doing so helps family members to value your opinion and trust your judgment.

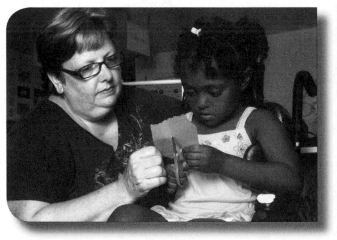

Even if you feel secure in the relationship that you have built with a family, approach them with care. An issue that may seem obvious to you might have gone completely unnoticed by parents. Even if family members suspect something, no one wants to hear from someone else that his or her child may have a special need. Being faced with this idea is a huge emotional strain, and many families flat out reject the notion right away. Do not be surprised or offended if they are skeptical or want a second opinion. Your concerns can bring up a variety of emotions and self-doubt in family members. They are probably worried about what the future holds for their child as well as for the rest of the family, and they may question their abilities as parents. Sometimes sharing your concerns is only planting the seed that there may be an issue. Most parents will need time to come to terms with the idea and act on it.

Below are some of the more common special needs identified in the toddler years.

| Motor Delays | ✿ weak or inconsistent reflexes<br>✿ slow to develop motor skills |
|---|---|
| Communication Delays | ✿ words not understood at expected age (misunderstood questions, trouble following directions)<br>✿ limited or no babbling<br>✿ sounds not made correctly at expected age<br>✿ has limited vocabulary for age |
| Visual Impairments | ✿ lack of interest in objects<br>✿ doesn't reach for or search out objects<br>✿ often bumps into things or trips |
| Hearing Impairments | ✿ lack of reaction to sounds<br>✿ surprised by "sudden appearance" of others<br>✿ babbling may begin, then stop |
| Emotional Disorders | ✿ unable to build or maintain relationships<br>✿ generally unhappy or depressed<br>✿ withdrawn<br>✿ behavior goes to extremes<br>✿ aggressive or self-injurious behaviors<br>✿ problems continue over a long period of time |

Early intervention is important no matter what issues you believe a child may have. Whatever their disabilities may be, these children also have many abilities. Early intervention builds upon these abilities and helps their young brains make important connections that will help these children to compensate as they grow.

## Meeting Toddlers' Needs

Once a professional has identified a toddler as having special needs, you may feel concerned and possibly overwhelmed. Try to think of this as simply background information or context in which to view the toddler. Do not define the child by his needs. Take the time to really understand him as an individual. It may take extra time and effort, depending on the child and the nature of his needs, but learn his strengths and interests as well as or better than you would those of any other child. This knowledge will be helpful when working with his family and caring for him.

A child with identified special needs may come to your program with an Individualized Family Service Plan (IFSP) already in place. This is a plan put together by a team that includes parents and specialists, educators, doctors and nurses, and social workers. It usually contains the child's current developmental information, general developmental goals, and specific objectives to meet those goals and evaluate progress. This plan can be very helpful to you. Not only will it help you to better understand the child's needs and abilities, but it can also be useful when thinking of ways to support the child in your program. If a toddler has recently been diagnosed as having special needs and does not have a plan, you may want to suggest to parents that they talk to their doctor or specialist about creating a plan.

Remember, you are not expected to be an expert, specialist, or therapist. Your job is to provide toddlers with a caring, nurturing environment that encourages them to grow, explore, and develop. Use the resources available to you to create an environment that is as nonrestrictive as possible. Try to ensure that a child with special needs has all the opportunities to participate in activities, develop relationships, and enjoy the experiences that are available to the other children in your program. After all, children with special needs are more similar to their peers than different. They enjoy and benefit from many of the same experiences.

Give yourself a break, and involve the people around you. Use family members as a resource. Chances are that they know quite a bit about their child's condition and needs. With the parents' permission, invite the child's specialists to your program. They may have important advice and insights on ways to make your program even more successful at meeting the needs of the special children in your care.

## Adapting Your Environment

Get a new perspective on your environment by looking at it through the eyes of the children with special needs. Be aware of texture and audio cues for children who have visual impairments. Can a child who is visually impaired orient himself by noticing that the floor changes from carpet to a hard surface as he moves from the play area to the food area? Can you play soft, soothing music in the quiet space to help him identify that area? Be aware of the acoustics of your space for children with hearing impairments. Too much background noise could make it hard for these children to focus on specific sounds. Children who are tactile-defensive are very sensitive to textures and touch sensations. They may become overwhelmed or upset by textures or tactile experiences that many children enjoy or experience without incident, including playing in sand, fingerpainting, or handling textured toys or certain fabrics. Can you provide tools to help children who are tactile-defensive explore these materials more comfortably? Also, if you have a child who uses a wheelchair or other special equipment, be sure that there is enough space to maneuver the equipment through your program.

There is a lot of equipment out there that is specifically designed for children with different disabilities. Much of this equipment can also be useful for children who may have less severe developmental issues. Bolsters (cylindrical cushions) and wedges are very helpful for positioning children who have difficulty sitting or lying on their stomachs or sides. These special cushions help to prop children up in a way that encourages them to explore and develop their skills. Consider other items:

- Gloves, sticks, and paintbrushes for children who are tactile-defensive
- Large crayons and markers or even Velcro straps for children with fine motor issues

## Being an Effective Caregiver

To be an effective caregiver of a child with special needs, learn as much as you can about the child and his condition. Remember to use parents as a resource. Ask them to recommend resources to help you learn more. Most important, keep the lines of communication wide open. It is important that you work as a team with family members and the other professionals in the child's life. The more you learn about the child, the more successful you will be in addressing his needs. Adapt your program, but avoid overprotecting the child. Just like all children, those with special needs need to be challenged and have opportunities to problem solve without getting too frustrated.

Caring for a child with special needs can be challenging. Recognize your own feelings. Acknowledging and talking about them with the other people you work with can help you to resolve or move past these feelings. Developing a strong relationship and supporting the growth and development of a child with special needs—or any child—is very rewarding. Each milestone, every small achievement brings with it great joy and a sense of accomplishment for the child, for his family, and for you.

# Resources

Dombro, A. L., Colker, L. J., and Trister Dodge, D. 1999. *The creative curriculum for infants and toddlers*. Bethesda, MD: Teaching Strategies, Inc.

Gonzalez-Mena, J., and Widmeyer Eyer, D. 2008. *Infants, toddlers, and caregivers*. Columbus, OH: McGraw-Hill.

Greenman, J., and Stonehouse, A. 2002. *Prime times: A handbook for excellence in infant and toddler care*. St. Paul, MN: Redleaf Press.

National Association for the Education of Young Children. 2007. *NAEYC early childhood program standards and accreditation criteria: The mark of quality*. Washington, DC: National Association for the Education of Young Children.

National Center for Infants, Toddlers, and Families. www.zerotothree.org

National Institute for Child and Human Development. *Positional plagiocephaly*. Retrieved on July 12, 2011, from http://www.nichd.nih.gov/health/topics/positional_plagiocephaly.cfm

U.S. Department of Education. *Building the Legacy: IDEA 2004*. http://idea.ed.gov

Willis, C. 2009. *Teaching infants, toddlers, and twos with special needs*. Silver Spring, MD: Gryphon House, Inc.

# Activities

**To help you create learning experiences that support the development of the toddlers in your care, the remainder of this book is devoted to developmentally appropriate and engaging activity experiences. As you flip through the various activities, think about the ages and developmental interests of the toddlers in your care. Do you have a child who loves to explore textures? Perhaps one of the toddlers is on the verge of speaking and you'd like to provide an experience that will encourage this. Look for activities that fit the developmental ages and unique interests of individual children.**

The activities are divided according to developmental area and go in chronological order according to age to help you quickly find activities that will meet the interests and ages of the children in your care. Remember, all children develop at different rates, so it is not uncommon to have a 24-month-old child who is interested in the language activities designed for a 12-month-old, but the motor activities for an 18-month-old. You will also notice that each activity provides a brief explanation of its benefits. All of the activity experiences in this book list multiple areas of development in the Benefits section because toddler development is so interconnected. Do not be surprised if a child is particularly interested in one area or aspect of the activity over the others. This is common.

In addition to an explanation of the activity and its benefits, each also includes information about what to look for as you watch a child engage in the activity experience. These questions help to focus your attention on key expectations of child engagement and can help you to understand how an individual child is working through the developmental milestones. Finally, each activity includes a "tips" section you will find useful to help you modify the activity for different ages, abilities, or interests.

# Floor Catch

## What to do

1. Sit across from a toddler with your legs spread out to keep the ball from rolling too far away.
2. Gently roll the ball to the child.
3. Encourage him to push it back toward you.
4. Continue for as long as he remains interested.

## What to look for

✿ Does the child anticipate the ball's approach?
✿ After being shown how to push the ball, does he push it on his own?

## Tips

✿ Vary the speed at which you push the ball. Does the child react?
✿ With older toddlers, you can explore using two or three balls at once. Keeping up with the balls that you roll will encourage hand-eye coordination and promote concentration skills.

**Social and Emotional** ☺☹

**12+ months**

**Indoors**

**Prep Time** 🕐 **None**

**Benefits**
✿ Promotes social interaction
✿ Develops gross motor skills

**Materials**
☑ Ball or rolling rattle

# Here I Am!

## What to do

1. Cover each photo with contact paper on both sides.
2. Fasten a large magnet to the back of each photo using a hot glue gun.
3. Place the bin of photo magnets near the metal surface.
4. Invite children to find their photos in the bin and stick them to the metal surface.

## What to look for

✿ Does the child recognize herself in the photo? Does she recognize others?

✿ Is the child able to add and remove her magnet independently?

## Tips

✿ Make this a morning sign-in ritual. As children post their pictures, talk with them about other children who are here and those who are missing.

✿ Name different children, and encourage a child to look for the appropriate pictures.

✿ If you want to avoid using magnets, try Velcro or felt on a fabric board.

---

**Social and Emotional** ☺☹

**12+ months**

**Indoors**

**Prep Time** ⏲ **25 minutes**

**Benefits**

✿ Encourages positive self-esteem

✿ Promotes awareness of others

✿ Promotes fine motor skills

**Materials**

☑ Photo of each child

☑ Clear contact paper

☑ Hot glue gun (adult use only)

☑ Old magnets or magnetic strips (use only large magnets to avoid a choking hazard)

☑ Magnetic surface at a child's height (whiteboard, refrigerator, or old cookie sheet)

☑ Bin for storing photo magnets

# Feel Better

## What to do

1. When a child in the group is injured or upset, as you comfort the child, involve other children.
2. Encourage other children to help. Ask them to bring the upset child a favorite toy or blanket, or show them how to rub the child's back and give words of comfort.
3. Acknowledge and thank the children for their help.

## What to look for

✿ How do the other children react to the upset child?
✿ Do the children begin to comfort friends independently?
✿ How does the upset child respond to the help of his peers?

## Tips

✿ Encourage pretend play by acting distressed yourself or having a stuffed animal cry. Help children think of ways to comfort the stuffed animal.
✿ Label specific feelings. Move beyond sad and mad. Verbalize feelings of frustration, disappointment, and so on.

**Social and Emotional** ☺☹

**12+ months**

**Anywhere**

**Prep Time** ⏱ **None**

**Benefits**
✿ Develops empathy
✿ Promotes social skills
✿ Fosters self-esteem

**Materials**
☑ None

# Little Helper

Social and Emotional ☺☹

18+ months

Anywhere

Prep Time ⏱ None

Benefits
✿ Encourages cooperation
✿ Develops self-esteem
✿ Promotes listening skills

Materials
☑ None

## What to do

1. Ask children to help you with different tasks throughout the day.
2. Begin with specific and simple one-step directions such as, "Please take the napkins to the table," or "Please put your blocks in the block bin." Older children can handle two-step directions such as, "Please wipe the table, and put the towel in the sink."
3. Be sure to model the language you want children to develop. Ask for help with a please, and be sure to thank each child.

## What to look for

✿ Is the child able to follow a simple instruction?
✿ Does he enjoy helping?

## Tips

✿ Invite a child who is having a bad day to be your special helper.
✿ Make chores a part of the daily routine. Give children the same responsibilities over a long period of time. Jena may water plants in the morning, while Chris always puts out the napkins for snack.
✿ Toddlers love transporting things. Invite them to help you move objects by pulling the items in carts or carrying them. Be sure that any instructions you give are very specific and simple to follow.

# Visiting Vehicles

## What to do

1. Invite two or more children to sit with you.
2. Start with one car. Push it to a child sitting next to you.
3. Encourage that child to push it to the next child.
4. Keep passing the car around the group for as long as the children are interested.

## What to look for

✿ Do the children pass the car along when asked?
✿ Do they begin to realize they will get the car back after passing it?
✿ Do the children enjoy interacting with friends through this sharing game?

## Tips

✿ If, after a moment of playing with the car and some prompting from you, a child is not willing to pass it along, don't reprimand the child, he simply may not be developmentally ready for sharing yet. Let him continue playing with the truck and bring out another car or truck to continue the game. The reluctant child may eventually want to join in the game again, but it should be the child's choice.
✿ Put words to what the children are doing. Use directional or motion words to describe how the car is moving. Describe who is passing the car to whom, and so on.
✿ Encourage children, especially those with limited speech, to make car or truck noises as they roll the vehicle to a friend.
✿ If you need to stop the activity before children are ready, give them a concrete warning, such as, "We have time to pass the car two more times, then we have to stop." Count down from two with the children.

**Social and Emotional** ☺☹

**18+ months**

**Anywhere**

**Prep Time** ⏱ **5 minutes**

**Benefits**
✿ Develops sharing skills
✿ Promotes gross motor development

**Materials**
☑ Several toy cars or trucks

# Sounds of Home

## What to do

1. Invite a family member to come in with one of his child's favorite books and be recorded reading it.
2. Try to find a copy of each book that is recorded.
3. Play the recording for the child, and invite the child to look through the book while listening.
4. Do this for each child in your program.

## What to look for

- Does the child respond to the sound of her family member's voice?
- If it is available, does the child seek out or flip through the corresponding book?

## Tips

- Take a photo of each family member, and print a copy of the book cover. Make these into cards and make them available in the reading and quiet area so that children refer to them as a way to ask to listen to these recordings.
- Invite family members to come in as guest storytellers to read a story you have in the classroom.
- Use this activity to help children transition from nap time.

**Social and Emotional** ☺☹

**18+ months**

**Anywhere**

**Prep Time** 🕐 **15 minutes**

**Benefits**
- ✿ Promotes emotional well-being
- ✿ Encourages home-school cooperation
- ✿ Develops language

**Materials**
- ☑ Favorite book
- ☑ Recording device

# Dancing Ribbons

## What to do

1. Knot the middle of each ribbon to the ring so that you have two tails of approximately equal lengths.
2. Play the music. Hold the ring so that the ribbons move and wave as you dance.
3. Encourage the child to hold the ring and move to the music.

## What to look for

✿ Does the child show interest in the movement of the ribbons?

✿ Is he able to hold and manipulate the ring purposefully?

✿ Does the he move in rhythm to the music?

## Tips

✿ Try this activity in front of a mirror so that children can watch themselves dance and the ribbons move.

✿ Encourage small groups of children to dance together.

✿ If only one or two children are interested in the ring of ribbons, add an additional motor element by moving the ring above and around the child or children. Encourage them to reach, stretch, twist, and grab for it.

✿ If you need to stop this activity before children are ready, give them a warning. Set a visual timer where children can see it. When the timer rings, the activity stops.

Social and Emotional ☺☹

18+ months

Anywhere

Prep Time ⏱ 10 minutes

**Benefits**

✿ Encourages self-expression

✿ Develops fine and gross motor skills

✿ Promotes sensory development (visual, tactile, auditory)

**Materials**

☑ Medium-sized ring (stiff bracelet, plastic lid with center removed and wrapped in tape, and so on)

☑ Several ribbons (about one-foot lengths)

☑ Music

# If You're Happy...

## What to do

1. Begin singing:

   *If you're happy and you know it, clap your hands.*
   *(clap hands together)*
   *If you're happy and you know it, clap your hands.*
   *(clap hands together)*
   *If you're happy and you know it and you really want to show it,*
   *If you're happy and you know it, clap your hands.*
   *(clap hands together)*

2. Invite the children to sing with you.
3. Repeat several times to give the children a chance to get the hang of it.

## What to look for

- Do the children clap with you?
- Do the children begin to understand and sing the lyrics?
- Do they begin singing spontaneously?

## Tips

- Try out different verses, for example, if you're mad… stomp your feet; if you're sad…wipe your tears; if you're silly…spin around; and so on.
- When children are expressing their feelings in unhealthy ways (hitting, biting), remind them of the appropriate verse of the song. If they're mad, invite them to stomp their feet!
- Make a picture card that represents this song, and make it available to children in a song box or basket to use when they would like to ask you to sing this song.

**Social and Emotional** ☺☹

**24+ months**

**Anywhere**

**Prep Time** ⏱ **None**

**Benefits**
- Promotes positive expression of emotions
- Develops vocabulary
- Develops gross motor skills

**Materials**
- ☑ None

# Let's Pretend

## What to do

1. Use the utility knife to cut windows and a door into a large cardboard box. When turned upside-down, this box will be your house or store.
2. Set the box out for the children. In and around the box, place a variety of household items.
3. Invite children to play.

## What to look for

✿ Do the children imitate adults doing household tasks?
✿ Do the children interact and play cooperatively?

## Tips

✿ Create prop boxes for more pretend play, for example, a doctor's office, a grocery store, and so on.
✿ Cut squares from contact paper, peel them as you give them to each child and invite children to decorate the house. Remember, it's the process of decorating that is important for the children. They don't need the house to look perfect.
✿ Make dress-up items available for more pretend fun.
✿ If children have a hard time cleaning up after this activity, make cleanup into a game. Use a flashlight to point out items that need to be picked up. Use the light to guide children to the place where each item is stored.

---

**Social and Emotional** ☺☹

**24+ months**

**Anywhere**

**Prep Time** ⏱ **15 minutes**

**Benefits**
✿ **Develops social skills**
✿ **Promotes language development**

**Materials**
☑ **Variety of household items (preferably toddler-sized), for example phone, broom, dishes, empty food boxes, and so on**
☑ **Large cardboard box (ask for them at a local retail store)**
☑ **Utility knife (for adult use only)**

# Flannel Board Tots

## What to do

1. For each photo, cut out the body of each child.
2. Using each photo cutout as a template, cut a piece of felt for a backing.
3. Glue the felt backing to the back of the photo. Set aside to dry.
4. Use the felt photo dolls with a flannel board. You or the children may use them to talk about parts of the body, tell stories, act out situations, and so on.

## What to look for

❀ Do the children recognize their own images? Do they recognize the images of others?
❀ Do the children use the cutouts in imaginative play?

## Tips

❀ You may also want to use the felt photo dolls and flannel board as part of a sign-in routine or to assign chores.
❀ Use the photo dolls to help children work through difficult emotions or situations. If there is a conflict between two children, revisit the situation once the child or children are calm by reenacting the situation with the photo dolls. Talk about how each child might have felt during the conflict, and act out other choices the children could have made. Encourage the children to participate as much as possible.

**Social and Emotional** ☺☹

**24+ months**

**Anywhere**

**Prep Time** ⏱ **20 minutes**

**Benefits**
❀ Encourages self-expression
❀ Promotes self-esteem
❀ Develops language skills

**Materials**
☑ Large (at least 4" x 6") full-body photos of each child
☑ Felt
☑ Scissors
☑ Glue
☑ Flannel board

# Dancing Buddies

## What to do

1. Play music.
2. Encourage pairs of children to hold hands as they move to the music.
3. Get involved! Dance with a child, or join a pair.

## What to look for

- ✿ Are the children able to coordinate dancing and holding hands?
- ✿ Do they enjoy dancing with others?

## Tips

- ✿ Try this activity when children have to wait. Sing a song, and encourage them to dance to it while holding hands.
- ✿ Experiment with music of different tempos. Slowly turn down the volume to get children to settle down or sit down.
- ✿ Turn the dancing into follow the leader, to get children to line up or move from one space to another.

**Social and Emotional** ☺☹

**30+ months**

**Anywhere**

**Prep Time** ⏲ **None**

**Benefits**
- ✿ Encourages self-expression
- ✿ Promotes positive social interaction
- ✿ Develops gross motor skills

**Materials**
- ☑ Music

# Where Is Wendy?

## What to do

Sing to the tune of "Frère Jacques":

> *Where is Wendy? (replace with child's name)*
> *Where is Wendy?*
> *Here she is! Here she is! (child stands)*
> *I'm glad you're here today, ma'am, (substitute sir for boys)*
> *Let me shake your hand, ma'am, (shake child's hand)*
> *Now sit right down. (child sits)*

## What to look for

✿ Does the child respond to her name in the song?
✿ After hearing the song several times, does she react with the appropriate movements?

## Tips

✿ The first few times you do this activity with children, you may want to model the expected behaviors by asking another adult to join you in the circle and call out that person's name first. You can also use yourself as the first example.

✿ Do not force a large group of children to sit through this song. Instead, sing the song with one or two children, and encourage other interested children to come and join you.

✿ Try this activity as a way to help older toddlers become familiar with the circle-time routines they are likely to encounter as they move on to preschool.

✿ Experiment with different lyrics for different times of day.

**Social and Emotional** ☺☹

**30+ months**

**Anywhere**

**Prep Time** ⏱ **None**

**Benefits**
✿ Develops language
✿ Promotes positive self-esteem

**Materials**
☑ None

# Baby Signs

## What to do

1. Use sign language or make up simple gestures to represent common words such as juice, more, hungry, wet, and so on (for pictures of suggested signs, see the next page).
2. Introduce one sign at a time by using the gesture every time you say the word.
3. When the child begins to use the gesture, give him positive reinforcement by immediately letting him know that you understand what he is communicating.
4. Slowly add more words to the child's sign vocabulary.

## What to look for

✿ Is the child able to mimic the signs you have created?
✿ Does he communicate with signs?
✿ Does he begin to create his own signs? Be on the lookout for this, and incorporate his signs into your vocabulary!

## Tips

✿ Encourage other staff and family members to use these signs with the child.
✿ Create name signs for the children in your group.
✿ Signing and gestures enable children to communicate successfully long before their vocal cords and muscle control allow them to talk. Rather than delaying speech, signing seems to encourage communication, which can lead to early speech and improved vocabulary.

Language

12+ months

Anywhere

**Prep Time** ⊘ None

**Benefits**
✿ Develops vocabulary
✿ Encourages communication
✿ Develops fine motor skills

**Materials**
☑ None

# Baby Signs

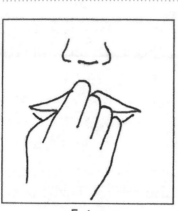

**Eat**

Hand places food in mouth.

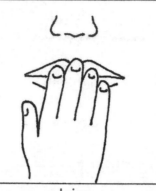

**Juice**

Fingers tap mouth.

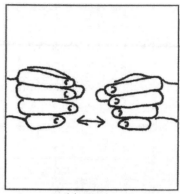

**More**

Fingers and thumbs pinched together. Touch fingertips together.

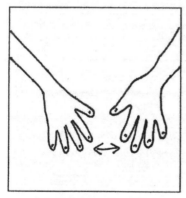

**All Done**

Hands shake back and forth.

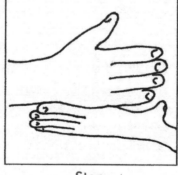

**Stop**

Edge of one hand comes down on palm.

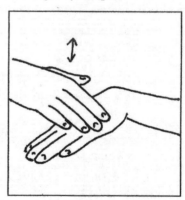

**Hurt**

Fingers of one hand tap the back of the other.

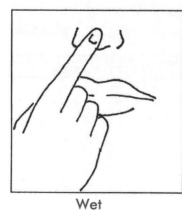

**Wet**

Index finger touches nose.

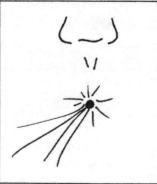

**Hot**

Blow gently.

**Out**

Elbow bent, finger points away from body.

# Pack It Up

## What to do

1. Set out an open suitcase, and begin packing the familiar objects.
2. When children approach to see what you are doing, explain that you would like some help packing some things into the suitcase.
3. Ask a child to bring you a familiar, nearby item. Use directional words, for example, "Niko, please bring me the doll lying next to the cradle."
4. Thank the child for the item, and put the item in the suitcase.
5. Continue asking for specific items for as long as children remain interested.

## What to look for

❀ Is the child able to identify the item you named?
❀ Does the child respond to your directions?
❀ Does he help you place the items in the suitcase?

## Tips

❀ To build vocabulary, pack up related items, for example, clothes, animals, and so on.
❀ Use a puppet as the packer. Children often respond well to puppets. The puppet can help the child find an item if he is having trouble.
❀ Unpack the bag, and name each item as you remove it.
❀ Try this activity with boxes or baskets at cleanup time.

**Language** ❀

**12+ months**

**Anywhere**

**Prep Time** ⏲ **10 minutes**

**Benefits**
✿ **Develops language and vocabulary**
✿ **Encourages cooperation**

**Materials**
☑ **Bag, box, or suitcase**
☑ **Items to pack**

Irvington Public Library
Irvington-on-Hudson, NY

ACTIVITIES

# Animal Sounds

## What to do

As you look at pictures of animals with a toddler, name the animal and make the sound the animal makes.

## What to look for

- Does the child imitate the animal sound? Can she name the animal?
- Does the child begin to associate the animals' pictures with their sounds?

## Tips

- Add a movement component. Show the child how the animal moves, and encourage her to imitate you.
- Use stuffed animals or plastic animals rather than pictures.
- Take a trip to a zoo to see the real animals. Be sure to make the visit short and sweet.
- Animal sounds are a fun way to encourage children with emerging speech to practice common sound patterns, but other sounds such as car or truck noises and sound effects are equally effective at building skills. Explore different sounds based on children's individual interests.

Language

12+ months

Anywhere

Prep Time ⏱ 5 minutes

Benefits
- Develops language
- Encourages the imitation of sound for speech

Materials
- ☑ Pictures of animals

# Picture Cards

## What to do

1. Use the contact paper to laminate individual pictures of familiar items onto the index cards.
2. Place the pictures in a basket, and make them available to the children.
3. Invite children to empty the basket and look at the pictures.
4. Talk about or name the items as the children look at them.
5. Encourage them to point to items that you name.

## What to look for

✿ Does the child name the item pictured?
✿ How else does he use the picture cards?

## Tips

✿ Try to find images of items with no background, or cut the background away to reduce the visual clutter for children.
✿ Make a matching game with older children by using pictures of items in the room. They can match the pictures to real objects.
✿ Have different groups of cards, for example, animal cards, toy cards, people cards, and so on.

**Benefits**
✿ Builds vocabulary

**Materials**
☑ Pictures of familiar items cut out of magazines
☑ Index cards
☑ Clear contact paper
☑ Basket to store pictures

# Can You Find It?

## What to do

1. Glue several (4–6) images of items in the room onto individual index cards.
2. Collect the objects, and put them in a basket.
3. Look at the cards with a child. Encourage children to name each item, find it in the basket, and place the item and the card together.
4. If he does not know the word for the item, name the item for him.

## What to look for

✿ Is the child able to identify a real-life item from a picture?
✿ Is he able to name the items pictured?
✿ Does he enjoy hunting for the items pictured?

## Tips

✿ For another variation, name an item, and encourage the child to point to its picture card.
✿ Create several card groupings (animal cards, clothing cards, vehicle cards, and so on).
✿ Liven up the game by using the cards and objects to create a scavenger hunt.

**Language** ✿

**18+ months**

**Anywhere**

**Prep Time** ⏱ **15 minutes**

**Benefits**
✿ **Develops language**
✿ **Promotes object and symbol correspondence**

**Materials**
☑ **Index cards**
☑ **Pictures (photos or images cut from catalogs) of several small items in the room**
☑ **Glue**
☑ **Basket**

# Book Nook

## What to do

1. Sit in a cozy place with a variety of books close by.
2. Invite a child to choose a book and sit with you.
3. Look through the book together. Encourage the child to talk about the pictures.
4. Read the story if the child seems interested, but do not force it. Enjoying time with a book is more important.

## What to look for

✿ Is the child able to turn the pages?
✿ Does she identify items pictured?
✿ Does she enjoy listening to the story?

## Tips

✿ Make book time as enjoyable and interactive as possible. Take your time. Invite the child to make the sounds of animals or objects pictured. Encourage her to "read" to you.

✿ After reading a story to older children, talk about it. Ask children which parts they liked. Can they express their thoughts? Do they retell important events?

**Language** 🗣

**18+ months**

**Anywhere**

**Prep Time** ⏱ **5 min**

**Benefits**
✿ Promotes reading
✿ Encourages bonding
✿ Develops language

**Materials**
☑ Variety of books

# Tell Me a Story

## What to do

1. When with a child, begin telling a story that directly involves the child. For example, when snuggling a toddler who is having difficulties transitioning, begin telling the child about how you imagine his day has been. "I'll bet this morning you woke up very sleepy still and ate waffles for breakfast. Is that right?"
2. Give the child opportunities to be involved in the storytelling and respond as often as possible.
3. Continue with the story, "And then you got dressed in your favorite shirt...I'm pretty sure this is your favorite shirt...and then you came here and now we are snuggling. But soon you are going to climb down from my lap and head over to the pretend kitchen area, because I see you playing there a lot. I wonder what you are going to cook up over there today? Maybe a feast for our lunch?"
4. Feel free to get creative and silly in your storytelling. For example, you might tell a story about a dream you had about the child performing in a circus act or living in the jungle with a family of monkeys, and so forth. No matter what story you decide to tell, be sure to invite the child to participate in the telling by asking questions and incorporating the child's ideas.

## What to look for

* Does the child listen attentively and understand your basic story?
* Does he answer questions appropriately?
* Does he enjoy being involved as a character or participant in the storytelling?

**Language**

**18+ months**

**Anywhere**

**Prep Time** ⏲ **None**

**Benefits**
* **Promotes vocabulary**
* **Encourages sequential thinking**
* **Develops language**

**Materials**
* ☑ **None**

## Tips

* Make storytelling time as enjoyable and interactive as possible. Add details about the sights, sounds, and smells in the story. Include sound effects and invite the child to make them with you.
* Tell and retell the same stories. Don't worry about making all of the details the same. See how much of the story the child remembers.
* Look for interesting pictures or images that you can use to inspire a story. Look for picture books at your local library that do not have text. Your local librarian can help you find such books. Then tell your own story around the pictures.

# My Day Book

## What to do

1. Place the photos in a photo book, or make your own photo book by laminating the photos, 2 or 3 to a page, onto the poster paper.
2. With the hole punch, make 2 or 3 holes along one side of each page.
3. Bind the pages together by looping the yarn through the holes.
4. Make the book available to the children.

## What to look for

- Do the children identify themselves or others in the photos?
- Do they talk about their memories of that day?

## Tips

- Write captions for the photos you include in the book, and make the book available for family members to look at as well.
- When you look at the book with a child, talk about your memories, and ask the child questions about that day.
- If you do not have contact paper, use self-sealing sandwich bags to protect the photos. Staple them together or use a hole punch and yarn to create the binding.

**Language**

**24+ months**

**Anywhere**

**Prep Time** ⏱ **20 minutes**

**Benefits**
- Develops vocabulary
- Promotes understanding of the concept of time (past)

**Materials**
- ☑ Photos of children taken on a particular day (field trip, class visitor, ordinary day)
- ☑ Commercially available photo book, or make your own with
  - ◆ Cardboard or poster paper
  - ◆ Clear contact paper
  - ◆ Hole punch
  - ◆ Yarn

# It's a Zoo!

## What to do

1. Show children an animal picture or toy animal.
2. Name the animal, or invite children to name it.
3. Encourage the children to move and make sounds like the animal.
4. Continue with other animal pictures.

## What to look for

✿ Can the children identify the animals pictured?
✿ How do they choose to move or sound?

## Tips

✿ Use this activity during transition times. Invite children to be quiet as mice, or ask a child to move like a bunny to the changing table, and so on.
✿ Make a video or audio tape of the children acting like animals, then play it back for them.
✿ Begin with familiar animals, then introduce children to new ones.
✿ Connect this activity to animal songs you may know, such as "Baa, Baa Black Sheep" or "Itsy Bitsy Spider."

**Language** ✿

**24+ months**

**Anywhere**

**Prep Time** ⏲ **5 minutes**

**Benefits**
✿ Develops speech and vocabulary
✿ Encourages imaginative play
✿ Develops gross motor skills

**Materials**
☑ Pictures of animals or animal toys
*Note: Toddlers are concrete thinkers and may respond better to three-dimensional representations of animals (toy animals) than to two-dimensional pictures.*

# Class Song File

## What to do

1. Glue or draw a picture representing a class song onto each index card.
2. Place the index cards in a file box, and make the box accessible to children.
3. When a child chooses a song from the class song file, sing the song with the child.

## What to look for

✿ Does the child initiate the search for a song?
✿ Does the child join in the singing or movements?

## Tips

✿ Give each child a chance to choose a song to sing with you or the group.
✿ Turn things around, and challenge children to find or point to the card that represents the song you are singing.
✿ Name the items pictured or colors featured on the cards.

**Language** 🗣

**24+ months**

**Anywhere**

**Prep Time** ⏱ **20 minutes**

**Benefits**

✿ **Encourages communication**
✿ **Promotes sound and symbol correspondence**

**Materials**

☑ **Index cards**
☑ **Pictures representing class songs, cut from magazines or drawn (a school bus for "The Wheels on the Bus," and so on)**
☑ **Glue**
☑ **Index card file box**

# Following My Words

## What to do

1. Give a child silly directions to follow. Start with something simple, such as, "Touch your nose," or "Jump up and down."
2. Gradually make the directions more complex by stating two or more things to do, "Spin around, and then sit down."
3. Continue for as long as the child remains interested.

## What to look for

* Does the child follow your directions?
* Does he give you directions to follow?

## Tips

* Encourage children to give you silly directions to follow.
* Promote social interactions by bringing a few children together to do this activity.
* Mix silly directions with actual things you would like he child to do, such as "Spin around. Wiggle your fingers, and then take off your coat."
* Try this as a transition-time activity. It is especially helpful when children are waiting.

**Language**

**24+ months**

**Anywhere**

**Prep Time** ⏱ **None**

**Benefits**
* Develops listening skills
* Promotes language
* Encourages motor development

**Materials**
☑ None

# What Is This For?

## What to do

1. Pick up or point out any nearby item, and ask a child, "What is this for?"
2. Listen to the explanation the child gives.
3. Repeat the child's explanation using correct grammar and more sophisticated wording if necessary.

## What to look for

✿ Is the child able to get across his ideas in words?

✿ Does the child come up with creative explanations?

## Tips

✿ Remember, the goal is for the child to think about the object and verbalize his thoughts rather than to come up with one correct response.

✿ If a child is reluctant to participate, get silly! Make up a silly use for the object that you are holding, such as, "I think this spoon might be used for brushing my hair!" Then ask the child what he thinks it might be used for.

✿ When children ask you those unavoidable what and why questions, try turning the question around on them by asking, "What do you think?"

**Language** ✎

**30+ months**

**Anywhere**

**Prep Time** ⊕ **None**

**Benefits**
✿ Develops language

**Materials**
☑ Any nearby item

# What Are You Doing?

## What to do

1. When a child is involved in an activity, ask him open-ended questions such as, "What are you doing?" or "How did you think of that?"
2. Continue the conversation for as long as the child remains interested.

## What to look for

✿ Does the child respond to your questions appropriately?

✿ Is the child able to express his thoughts?

## Tips

✿ You can also promote language skills and self-esteem just by describing a child's actions. "I see you are putting the square green block on top of the tall orange block." It helps to increase the child's vocabulary and lets the child know that he is the center of your attention at the moment.

✿ If a child is filling a container or sorting objects, describe the colors of the objects he grabs, or count off the items as the child moves them.

✿ When toddlers ask you the why questions that they are famous for, turn the table on them and ask, "Why do you think?" Then listen to the creative responses they come up with!

**Language** 🗣

**30+ months**

**Anywhere**

**Prep Time** ⏲ **None**

**Benefits**
✿ **Develops vocabulary**
✿ **Promotes thinking skills**

**Materials**
☑ **None**

# Simple Sorting

## What to do

1. Set out a bowl of mixed items.
2. Invite a child to separate the cereal balls from the O-shaped cereal. Show the child how to place a cereal ball in one bowl and a cereal O in the other.

## What to look for

✿ Does the child successfully identify and separate the items?

## Tips

✿ Begin with only two items to sort. Introduce more items as the children get better at sorting.
✿ Make this a "helping" activity by encouraging children to separate toys that may have been mixed together (different sets of blocks, different types of puzzle pieces, and so on).
✿ Count off the items or point out attributes such as color, shape, or size as children sort them.

**Language** ✿

**30+ months**

**Anywhere**

**Prep Time** ⏱ **5 minutes**

**Benefits**
✿ Develops abstract thinking (categorizing) skills
✿ Promotes fine motor skills

**Materials**
☑ Items to sort (ball-shaped and O-shaped cereal, squares and circles, and so on)
☑ Bowls (one for mixed items, and one for each sorted item)

# Knees and Toes

## What to do

1. Begin singing:

   *Head, shoulders, knees and toes, knees and toes
   (point to each body part)
   Head, shoulders, knees and toes, knees and toes
   (point to each body part)
   Eyes and ears and mouth and nose (point to each
   body part)
   Head, shoulders, knees and toes, knees and toes
   (point to each body part)*

2. Invite the children to sing along with you.
3. Repeat several times to give the children a chance
   to get the hang of it.

## What to look for

✿ Do the children associate the lyrics with the actions?
✿ Do they enjoy the activity?

## Tips

✿ This is a great activity to do while children are
   waiting.
✿ Speed up or slow down the tempo of the song to
   change things up once the children catch on.
✿ Try out other body parts, such as arms, elbows, feet,
   and seat.
✿ Make mistakes on purpose, and see if the children
   point them out.

---

Language 🗣

30+ months

Anywhere

**Prep Time** ⏲ **None**

**Benefits**
✿ Develops vocabulary
✿ Promotes gross motor
   skills

**Materials**
☑ None

# Shake It Up!

## What to do

1. Serve a toddler a small helping of macaroni.
   **Note:** *Check for food allergies before this or any food-related activity.*
2. Show her how to shake out the cheese, and then give her the cheese shaker.
3. Encourage her to put cheese on her macaroni.
4. Remove the shaker and let her eat!

## What to look for

✿ Does the child successfully get cheese from the shaker?
✿ Does she show new interest in her food after helping to prepare it?
✿ Is she able to manipulate the spoon to eat?

## Tips

✿ If the toddler does not want to stop shaking out cheese, fill the shaker with only a small amount of cheese.
✿ Try this activity using applesauce and cinnamon sugar. Make sure the shaker has very small holes!
✿ Encourage other self-feeding activities, such as dipping bananas into yogurt.

Motor ✋

**12+ months**

**Meal Time**

**Prep Time** ⏱ **5 minutes**

**Benefits**
✿ **Develops gross motor skills**
✿ **Develops self-help skills**
✿ **Promotes understanding of cause and effect**

**Materials**
☑ **Grated cheese in a shaker**
☑ **Bowl of cooked macaroni**
☑ **Spoon**

# Stack 'Em Up!

## What to do

1. Set blocks out for a toddler to explore.
2. When the child picks up and sets down a block, show her how to stack by placing another block on top of it.
3. Encourage her to put another block on top of the block you stacked.
4. Continue for as long as the child is interested.

## What to look for

✿ Is the child able to successfully manipulate one block on top of another?
✿ Does she show pleasure in her accomplishment?
✿ Does she begin to stack blocks independently?

## Tips

✿ Make blocks of different textures or sizes available for toddlers to explore.
✿ If you are having trouble getting a toddler interested in the stacking game, place unexpected objects on the stack, like a toy car or animal figure. How does the child react? Laugh or otherwise show the child that you are being silly. Then invite her to try stacking, either with the silly object or with a block.

**Motor** 🖐

**12+ months**

**Anywhere**

**Prep Time** ⏲ **5 minutes**

**Benefits**
✿ **Develops fine motor skills**
✿ **Promotes understanding of cause and effect**

**Materials**
☑ **Blocks**

# Through the Tube

## What to do

1. Hold the tube near a toddler, and drop a small toy through it so that it comes out the other side. Continue doing this until the child reaches for it.
2. Hold the tube up for the child, and invite him to drop objects through or otherwise explore the tube. If the child is still actively exploring objects with his mouth, pay careful attention to ensure he does not ingest bits of the paper tube.

## What to look for

✿ Does this activity keep the child's attention?
✿ Does he experiment with different objects to put in the tube?
✿ What else does he do with the materials?

## Tips

✿ Try tubes of different sizes.
✿ Have a dowel rod or stick available to help children push objects through a longer tube.

**Motor** ✋

**12+ months**

**Anywhere**

**Prep Time** ⏲ **5 minutes**

**Benefits**
✿ Develops fine motor skills
✿ Promotes understanding of spatial relationships

**Materials**
☑ Paper towel tube
☑ Small toys to put through the tube (small cars, balls, scarves, and so on)

# Slide and Roll

## What to do

1. Set the rolling and sliding items near the slide.
2. Pick up something that will roll, and roll it down the slide to catch children's attention.
3. Invite the children to experiment with pushing different objects down the slide.

## What to look for

* Are the children aware of the difference between the way round objects or those with wheels move down the slide versus the way those without wheels move?
* How long do the children remain involved in the activity?
* How else do children experiment with either the slide or the objects?

## Tips

* Have different kinds of ramps available for the children (set at different angles, curved versus straight, and so on).
* Make this an art activity by first rolling the wheels of cars in tempera paint or even colored water and then rolling them across butcher paper.
* Use wrapping paper tubes with golf balls or small cars. The children can watch the cars disappear and then reappear out the bottom of the tube.

Motor 🖐

**18+ months**

**Anywhere**

**Prep Time** ⏱ **5 minutes**

**Benefits**
* Develops fine and gross motor skills
* Promotes understanding of cause and effect

**Materials**
☑ Variety of items that will roll (balls, circular blocks, small cars, and so on)
☑ Several items that will not roll (square blocks, stuffed animals, and so on)
☑ Ramp or slide

# Up, Down, In, Out

## What to do

1. Lay the ladder flat on the ground or use masking tape to lay out a ladder-shaped grid.
2. Invite children to walk or crawl in and out of the spaces between the ladder rungs.

## What to look for

✿ How do the children choose to move through the ladder rungs?
✿ Do the children enjoy exploring the ladder?

## Tips

✿ Try out different obstacles. Invite children to crawl through a tunnel of boxes, over a pile of cushions, and so on.
✿ Describe the child's movements, saying for example, "Tasha, look how you step right over the ladder rung."
✿ Use string or cut-out paper footprints to lay out a path through the ladder for children to follow.

**Motor** 🖐

**18+ months**

**Open Space**

**Prep Time** ⊘ **5 minutes**

**Benefits**
✿ Develops gross motor skills
✿ Promotes positive self-esteem

**Materials**
☑ Wooden ladder or masking tape

# Roller Painting

## What to do

1. Place a piece of paper in the dishpan so that the bottom is covered.
2. Dip a golf ball in tempera paint.
3. Place the golf ball on the paper in the dishpan.
4. Invite the child to tip the dishpan to make the ball roll across the paper.

## What to look for

- Is the child able to successfully manipulate the dishpan?
- Does the child notice the paint trail the ball leaves behind?

## Tips

- Have a container with water handy to hold the ball as you change the paper in the bin. While children's hands should stay clean during this activity, a damp towel may be useful to have on hand in case any decide to reach for the ball.
- Encourage children to experiment with other painting tools such as brushes, squeeze bottles, roller bottles, cotton swabs, and even straws to blow watery paint.
- Invite children to help clean up by giving them damp sponges or paper towels.

**Motor** ✋

**24+ months**

**Messy Area**

**Prep Time** 🕐 5 minutes

**Benefits**
- Develops fine motor skills
- Promotes understanding of cause and effect

**Materials**
- ☑ Golf ball (1 per child)
- ☑ Small plastic bin or dishpan (1 per child)
- ☑ Paper (1 piece per child)
- ☑ Tempera paint
- ☑ Smocks or old shirts to protect children's clothing

# Bottle Bowling

## What to do

1. Set up the soda bottles so that they are standing close together.
2. Roll the ball into the soda bottles, and watch them fall.
3. Set them up again.
4. Invite children to give it a try.

## What to look for

✿ Are the children able to successfully aim for the bottles?

✿ Do the children initiate the activity by setting up the bottles themselves?

✿ How else do the children use the balls and the bottles?

## Tips

✿ Use a large ball and bottles with younger children. Older children will enjoy the challenge of a smaller ball and bottles.

✿ Count the number of bottles children knock down, or count them as you set them up.

Motor 🖐

**24+ months**

**Indoors**

**Prep Time** ⏲ **5 minutes**

**Benefits**
✿ **Develops gross motor skills**
✿ **Promotes understanding of cause and effect**

**Materials**
☑ **Several empty plastic soda bottles**
☑ **Ball, preferably large**

# Pouring Pitchers

## What to do

1. Fill one pitcher about a third full of water.
2. Set the two pitchers out on the shallow tray.
3. Invite children to pour the water from one pitcher to the other, then back again.

## What to look for

✿ Are the children able to successfully pour the water from pitcher to pitcher?

## Tips

✿ Include a small sponge on the tray to encourage children to soak up spills.
✿ Set out a little bit of juice in small pitchers at snack time, and encourage children do their own pouring.
✿ Instead of water, put sand, rice, or beans in the pitchers. Have cups available for children to practice pouring.

**Motor** 🖐

**24+ months**

**Messy Area**

**Prep Time** ⏱ **5 minutes**

**Benefits**
✿ Develops fine motor skills
✿ Promotes eye-hand coordination
✿ Encourages self-help skills and self-esteem

**Materials**
☑ Two small pitchers
☑ Water
☑ Shallow tray

# Dancing Streamers

## What to do

1. Play the music, and give a streamer to each child.
2. Invite children to dance, run, and move with the streamers.

## What to look for

✿ Are the children interested in the movement of the streamers?

✿ How do they move? Do they use their whole bodies? Do they run? Jump? Twirl?

## Tips

✿ Do this activity where there are mirrors present. Encourage children to watch themselves move with the streamers.

✿ Take this activity outdoors on a day with a light wind.

✿ Play music of different tempos. Watch how the children react.

✿ If the streamers get torn or scattered about, make a clean-up game by wrapping masking tape, sticky side out, around each child's hand. Now they can "vacuum up" the papers just by touching them.

**Motor** 🖐

**24+ months**

**Open Space**

**Prep Time** 🕐 **5 minutes**

**Benefits**

✿ Develops gross motor skills

✿ Encourages creative expression

**Materials**

☑ Crepe paper streamers cut to two-foot lengths

☑ Music

# Balancing Path

## What to do

1. Use the tape or other item to mark a long, narrow path on the floor.
2. Walk along the path, always stepping on the tape as if it were a balance beam.
3. Invite children to do the same.

## What to look for

- Does the child follow the tape?
- Is the child able to stay on the tape and maintain her balance?
- Does she practice balancing on other objects?

## Tips

- For younger children, keep the path straight. Older children will enjoy the challenge of a twisting or spiraling path.
- Incorporate this activity into transition times. Make a line on the floor where you would like children to line up, or make a line through the building marking the children's path to the outdoors, and so on.
- Place a wood two-by-four flat on the ground to use as a low balance beam.

**Motor** 🖐

**30+ months**

**Anywhere**

**Prep Time** ⏲ **5 minutes**

**Benefits**
- Develops gross motor skills

**Materials**
- ☑ Masking tape, scarf, yarn, or other item for marking a path

# Making Mashed Potatoes

## What to do

1. Encourage children to wash and dry their hands before working with food.
2. Place the potatoes in the bowl, and invite children to take turns mashing them.
3. Ask a child or two to add the butter.
4. Pour some milk into the liquid measuring cup, and invite another child to pour the milk into the bowl with the potatoes.
5. Add salt to taste. Encourage the children to continue mashing.
6. Invite children to add more milk as needed.
7. Serve, eat, and enjoy!
   **Note:** *Check for food allergies before this or any food-related activity.*

## What to look for

✿ Do the children work cooperatively?
✿ Are they able to mash and pour successfully?

## Tips

✿ This activity works best in very small groups.
✿ Encourage children to help prepare other foods, spreading jam, scrambling eggs to be cooked by an adult, and so on.
✿ Give the children who are not actively mashing or pouring specific tasks, such as cutting the butter into smaller pieces, holding the bowl, setting the table, and so on.

---

**Motor** 🖐

**30+ months**

**Messy Area**

**Prep Time** ⏱ **25 minutes**

**Benefits**
✿ Develops fine and gross motor skills
✿ Encourages cooperation
✿ Promotes understanding of cause and effect

**Materials**
☑ Potatoes, cooked and peeled, but not hot
☑ Milk
☑ Butter, premeasured and cut
☑ Salt
☑ Bowl
☑ Liquid measuring cup
☑ Potato masher
☑ Serving plates or bowls
☑ Spoons

ACTIVITIES

# Grab It!

## What to do

1. Set out the small objects and the kitchen tongs.
2. Begin picking up the objects with the tongs.
3. Invite children to give it a try.

## What to look for

✿ Are the children able to manipulate the tongs?
✿ How else do they use the tongs?

## Tips

✿ Provide a bowl or jar that children can use to dump and fill using the tongs.
✿ For another variation, set out smaller objects and invite children to use spring-loaded clothespins. Make sure the springs are not too difficult for the children to open.
✿ Make cleanup fun by inviting children to pick up toys and put them away with the tongs.

**Motor** 🖐

**30+ months**

**Anywhere**

**Prep Time** ⏱ 5 minutes

**Benefits**
✿ Develops fine motor skills

**Materials**
☑ Simple spring-loaded kitchen tongs
☑ Small objects to pick up

# Over and Under

## What to do

1. Set the chairs a few feet apart with the backs facing each other.
2. Drape the sheet over the backs of the two chairs so that a ball can be tossed both over and under the sheet.
3. Stand or sit on one side of the sheet while a child stands on the other. Toss the ball back and forth. Describe whether you are throwing the ball over or under the sheet.

## What to look for

- Is the child able to catch and throw the ball successfully?
- Is the child able to differentiate between over and under?

## Tips

- Experiment with different ways to pass the ball back and forth: bounce it, roll it, and so on.
- Describe how you are passing the ball.
- Ask the child if he would like the ball to go over or under the sheet.

Motor ✋

30+ months

Anywhere

Prep Time ⏱ 5 minutes

**Benefits**
- Develops gross motor skills
- Promotes eye-hand coordination
- Builds vocabulary (directional words)

**Materials**
- ☑ Sheet or other cloth
- ☑ Two chairs
- ☑ Beanbag or soft ball

# Mold It, Mash It

## What to do

1. Set a toddler in a high chair or at a low table. Placing the child on the floor with a tray also works well. Give him a small portion of dough.
2. Encourage the toddler to explore, squish, and poke the dough. The dough will not harm him if ingested, but try not to let him bite off chunks.

## What to look for

❀ Does the child react to the texture?
❀ Is he able to manipulate the dough? Does he do so with his whole hand? Fingers?
❀ Does he have any other sensory responses? Is he interested in the smell? Taste?

## Tips

❀ If a toddler is not interested in grabbing the dough, set it on the table or tray. Flatten it a bit, and poke it with your fingers. Encourage him to put his fingers in the holes you have made.
❀ Make sure the child has a full belly to discourage him from eating the dough.
❀ Supervise younger children closely to prevent choking if they ingest bits of dough.
❀ Older toddlers may enjoy using simple tools such as sticks, mallets, or spoons to manipulate the dough.

**Sensory** 👂 👁

**12+ months**

**Messy Area**

**Prep Time** 🕐 **5 minutes**

**Benefits**
❀ Promotes tactile stimulation
❀ Develops fine motor skills

**Materials**
☑ Cloud Dough (see next page) or other oily playdough

# Cloud Dough

## What to do

1. Mix together the flour and oil.
2. Add the water, and knead the dough together. You may need more water to make the dough bind.
3. When the dough is smooth and oily, you are done!
4. Store it in an airtight container.

## Variations

✿ Add a small amount of food coloring for more visual appeal.

**Prep Time** ⏲ 10 minutes

**Ingredients**
3 cups flour
½ cup cooking oil
½ cup water

# Fingerpainting Fun

## What to do

1. Set a toddler in a high chair or at a low table.
2. Squeeze a small amount of paint onto the tabletop or tray.
3. Show the child how to move his fingers through the paint to make marks on the tray.
4. Encourage him to experiment and explore.

## What to look for

- How does the toddler react to the feel of the paint?
- How does he respond to the marks his fingers leave behind?

## Tips

- Have wet wipes or paper towels nearby to wipe the child clean before he moves on to another activity.
- Invite the child to help you clean up with a damp cloth or paper towels.
- Avoid using this activity with toddlers who are still actively exploring their environment with their mouths.

---

**Sensory**

**12+ months**

**Messy Area**

**Prep Time** ⏱ **5 minutes**

**Benefits**
- ✿ Promotes tactile stimulation
- ✿ Develops fine motor skills

**Materials**
- ☑ Nontoxic fingerpaint (one color)
- ☑ Large tray or tabletop

# Fingerpaint Recipe

**Prep Time** ⊕ **10 minutes**

**Ingredients**

1 cup flour
1 cup water
Food coloring
1/8 cup liquid dish
    detergent (optional)

## What to do

1. Place all ingredients in a bowl and stir. The dish detergent gives the paint a silky texture and makes cleanup a little easier, but it is not necessary. Leave it out if you are concerned about children ingesting the paint.
2. Use a handheld blender for very smooth paint, or stir it quickly with a spoon for a more bumpy texture.
3. Transfer the paint to a squeeze bottle, or store it in an airtight container and spoon it out as needed.

# Touch-and-Turn Wheel

## What to do

1. Tape the shapes onto the turntable.
2. Invite the children to touch the shapes and spin the turntable.

## What to look for

* Can children spin the turntable independently?
* Do they react to the various textures?

## Tips

* Have small toys handy for children to place on the turntable. Invite children to explore what happens to the toys when the turntable spins.
* Make different turntable patterns by arranging the shapes or items differently.

**Sensory** 👂 👁

**12+ months**

**Anywhere**

**Prep Time** 🕐 **20 minutes**

**Benefits**
* Promotes visual and tactile stimulation
* Develops fine motor skills
* Develops understanding of cause and effect

**Materials**
* ☑ Lazy Susan or kitchen turntable
* ☑ Tape
* ☑ Large shapes cut from textured items (sand paper, fabric, cotton batting, etc.)

# Sticky Paper Collage

## What to do

1. Secure the contact paper, sticky side up, to a wall or low table. You can fold over the top and bottom edges of the paper to make it stick, or use tape.
2. Set out the objects for sticking.
3. Stick a few items onto the contact paper, and invite children to help you.
4. Step back and watch the children explore the sticky surface and the textured items.

## What to look for

✿ Do the children enjoy exploring the sticky properties of the contact paper?

✿ Are they able to manipulate the small items to make them stick or to remove them from the contact paper?

## Tips

✿ If many children are interested in this activity, help them to spread out by providing several large sheets of contact paper.

✿ This activity is an excellent way to help children transition after nap time.

✿ Make collages with a theme, such as objects from nature, paper of a particular color, and so on.

✿ Make a clean-up game by wrapping masking tape, sticky side out, around each child's hand. Now they can "vacuum up" scraps and crumbs just by touching them.

**Sensory** 👂 👁

**18+ months**

**Indoors**

**Prep Time** ⏱ **10 minutes**

**Benefits**
✿ **Promotes tactile stimulation**
✿ **Develops fine motor skills**

**Materials**
☑ **Large piece of contact paper**
☑ **Variety of small pieces of paper or other light objects (tissue paper, construction paper, feathers, leaves, and so on)**

# Mood Music

## What to do

1. Decide the mood you would like to create, and select appropriate music.
2. Play the music, and watch children's reactions.

## What to look for

✿ How do the children react to the music? Does it affect their behavior?

## Tips

✿ Move to the music and encourage the children to move and dance with you.

✿ Provide props such as scarves or instruments to encourage movement or dramatic play.

✿ Use music purposefully to help children transition from active to quiet times. Songs and music can also help cue children and guide them through clean-up time or other difficult transitions.

**Sensory** 👂 👁

**18+ months**

**Anywhere**

**Prep Time** 🕐 **5 minutes**

**Benefits**

✿ Promotes auditory stimulation

✿ Encourages awareness of feelings

**Materials**

☑ Music that will encourage a specific mood (soothing, happy, energetic, and so on)

# Glitter Bottle

## What to do

1. Put one or two teaspoons of glitter in the plastic bottle.
2. Fill the bottle with water.
3. Screw on the bottle cap and seal it with the hot glue gun.
4. Turn the bottle upside-down and watch the glitter sparkle and fall.
5. Give the bottle to a child to explore.

## What to look for

✿ How does the child react to the sparkling glitter?
✿ Is the child able to manipulate the bottle?

## Tips

✿ Make a glitter bottle of "sleeping dust" for each child. Hand them out at nap time. This quiet activity will help children to relax and self-soothe.
✿ Experiment with colored water, or try an oil-and-water mixture instead of glitter.
✿ Use the glitter bottle to help children calm down and transition from active to quiet activities.

**Sensory** 👂 👁

**18+ months**

**Anywhere**

**Prep Time** ⏱ **10 minutes**

**Benefits**
✿ Promotes visual stimulation
✿ Encourages fine motor development

**Materials**
☑ Small clear plastic bottle
☑ Glitter
☑ Water
☑ Hot glue gun (adult use only)

# Scrub-a-Dub

## What to do

1. Fill the bucket or water table one-third full of warm water. Add soap.
2. Dip the sponges in the warm soapy water, and invite children to wash the items you have provided.
3. When the children are finished washing an item, they can set it out on the towels to dry.
4. Supervise closely. Never leave a child unattended around water!

## What to look for

- How do the children react to the feel of the soapy water?
- Are they involved with the task?

## Tips

- Do not rush the children as they wash and play with the water. Remember, it is the process that matters!
- Make this a regular routine. Once a week, invite children to help clean toys and tables in the classroom; after all, they do love to help!

**Sensory** 👂 👁

**18+ months**

**Messy Area**

**Prep Time** 🕐 **5 minutes**

**Benefits**
- ✿ **Promotes tactile stimulation**
- ✿ **Develops understanding of cause and effect**
- ✿ **Encourages self-help skills**

**Materials**
- ☑ **Water**
- ☑ **Large bucket, washbasin, or water table**
- ☑ **Dishwashing soap**
- ☑ **Sponges or cloths**
- ☑ **Items to wash (plastic toys, plastic dishes, and so on)**
- ☑ **Drying rack or drying towels**

# Shaving Cream Clouds

## What to do

1. Squirt a small amount of shaving cream on a table in front of each child.
2. Invite the children to touch, shape, and explore their shaving cream cloud.
3. When children are finished, give them a towel to wipe up what's left of their cloud.

   Note: *Use shaving cream only with children who are no longer actively exploring new objects with their mouths, and be aware of potential allergic reactions.*

## What to look for

✿ How does the child react to the texture and smell of the shaving cream?

✿ What does he do with his cloud?

## Tips

✿ If you are concerned about the children ingesting the shaving cream, whipped cream is a good substitute, although it does require more cleanup.

✿ Have conversations with children. Ask questions and talk about clouds or shaving cream. How does it smell? Feel?

✿ For a more interesting sensory experience, instead of squirting the shaving cream onto a tabletop, squirt it on water in the water-play table.

✿ Make this into a clean-up activity by squirting a small amount of shaving cream on tabletops or low windows. Children can "fingerpaint" them clean, then wipe them dry with paper towels.

**Sensory** 👂 👁

**18+ months**

**Messy Area**

**Prep Time** 🕐 **5 minutes**

**Benefits**

✿ **Promotes tactile and olfactory stimulation**

✿ **Develops fine motor skills**

**Materials**

☑ **Scented shaving cream**

☑ **Paper or cloth towel**

# Footprints

## What to do

1. Spread out the tarp near the mud. Have the washtub and towels nearby.
2. Invite children to remove their shoes and socks. Keep these items safely near the washtub and towels.
3. Encourage the children to step in the mud and then walk, skip, and drag their feet across the tarp.
4. Help children clean up by rinsing their feet in the washtub and drying them before putting socks and shoes back on.

## What to look for

- Do the children enjoy the sensation of the mud on their feet?
- How do they react to the marks they leave on the tarp?

## Tips

- Have only small groups of 2 to 3 children play in the mud at once.
- Encourage children to pay attention to their feet and footprints. Compare them.
- Have children make hand- and footprints on paper with tempera paint.

---

**Sensory** 👂 👁

**24+ months**

**Outdoors**

**Prep Time** ⏲ **5 minutes**

**Benefits**
- Promotes tactile stimulation
- Develops fine and gross motor skills

**Materials**
- ☑ Mud (or dirt and a hose)
- ☑ Large tarp or drop cloth
- ☑ Washtub and water for cleaning
- ☑ Towels

# Stuff Stamping

## What to do

1. Soak the rag in the tempera paint. Squeeze it out a just little, and place it in the tray. This is your stamp pad.
2. Cover a table with the butcher paper, and set out the tray and the objects for stamping.
3. Show children how to press an object to the stamp pad and then to the butcher paper.
4. Encourage them to stamp and experiment.

## What to look for

* Are the children able to do the stamping independently?
* Do they experiment with the different objects?

## Tips

* Minimize the mess by using only one color at a time. If you want to introduce another color, save the paper and stamp for another day.
* Children can also stamp on blacktop or a large chalkboard using a damp sponge and water.

---

**Sensory** 🦻 👁

**24+ months**

**Messy Area**

**Prep Time** 🕐 **5 minutes**

**Benefits**
* Promotes tactile and visual stimulation
* Develops fine motor skills
* Encourages understanding of cause and effect

**Materials**
☑ Watery tempera paint
☑ Old cloth or rag
☑ Shallow tray
☑ Butcher paper or other large sheet of paper
☑ 2 to 3 objects to stamp (celery stick, kitchen brush, paper cup, and so on)

# Herb Collage

## What to do

1. Secure a large piece of contact paper, sticky side up, to a low table by turning back the corners or taping the edges. Set out the herbs.
2. Invite children to place the herbs onto the contact paper to create a collage.
3. As the children handle the herbs, encourage them to sniff. Talk about the scents. Ask questions such as, "What do they remind you of?" and "Do they smell good or bad?"

## What to look for

✿ How do the children react to the smells and textures?
✿ Are they able to manipulate the herbs onto the contact paper?

## Tips

✿ Use clear contact paper. When the collage is finished, cover it with another layer of clear sticky paper to seal the design.
✿ Secure the contact paper to a wall for a slightly different experience.
✿ Use the same method to make a nature collage. Use leaves, grass, flowers, and so on.

Sensory 👂 👁

24+ months

Anywhere

Prep Time ⏲ 10 minutes

Benefits
✿ Promotes olfactory, visual, and tactile stimulation
✿ Develops fine motor skills

Materials
☑ Variety of fresh herbs (preferably with stems attached)
☑ Contact paper

# Fruit Fiesta

## What to do

1. Set the bowl in the center of a clean table.
2. Introduce the name of the fruit if the children are not familiar with it. If the fruit has peels or other inedible parts that are difficult for the children to remove, remove them yourself ahead of time.
3. Give each child a piece of fruit and a knife.
4. Invite children to explore the fruit. They may use their knives to cut the fruit into smaller pieces. They may smell the fruit, touch it, taste it, and so on. **Note:** *Check for food allergies before this or any other food-related activity.*

## What to look for

❀ How do the children react to the new fruit?
❀ Does this activity inspire conversation between the children?
❀ Do they use the utensils properly?

## Tips

❀ Talk about the experience with the children. Describe the colors, textures, flavors, and their actions.
❀ Older children can work together to make a fruit salad from a variety of different fruits that they cut up.

**Sensory** 👂 👁

**30+ months**

**Meal Time**

**Prep Time** ⏲ **10 minutes**

**Benefits**
❀ **Stimulates the senses**
❀ **Develops fine motor skills**

**Materials**
☑ **Whole fruit (enough for each child)**
☑ **Plastic knives (one per child)**
☑ **Small bowl (for peels and bad spots)**
☑ **Paper towels**

# What Made That Sound?

## What to do

1. Hide the instruments behind the screen so that children cannot see them.
2. Play one of the instruments.
3. Ask, "What's that sound?"
4. Remove the screen so that the instruments are in sight, and play each one.
5. Invite children to guess which instrument was the hidden instrument.
6. Continue with different instruments for as long as the children remain interested.

## What to look for

✿ Are the children able to differentiate among the different sounds the instruments make?
✿ Are they able to identify the hidden instrument being played?
✿ Do they begin to notice other sounds they encounter?

## Tips

✿ Make sure the children are familiar with the instruments you use in this activity. Begin the activity by inviting children to experiment and play with the instruments.
✿ For a variation on this activity, tape record familiar sounds: water running, a dog barking, a door closing, and so on. Play the tape for the children, and invite them to identify the sounds.
✿ Use specific sounds as transition cues. Ring a bell to signal snack time, or blow a whistle to start clean-up time.

**Sensory** 👂 👁

**30+ months**

**Anywhere**

**Prep Time** 🕐 **5 minutes**

**Benefits**

✿ **Promotes auditory stimulation**
✿ **Develops language skills**

**Materials**

☑ **Variety of musical instruments (drum, xylophone, maracas, and so on)**
☑ **Screen (divider, cardboard box, cloth, anything to hide instruments from view)**

# Water Painting

## What to do

1. Fill the spray bottles and buckets with water, and set out the painting materials.
2. Show children how they can use the water and painting materials to "paint" blacktop, cement, fences, buildings, climbing structures, and so on.
3. Invite the children to experiment and explore!
4. Supervise closely. Never leave a child unattended around water!

## What to look for

- ✿ How do the children manipulate the painting materials?
- ✿ Do they enjoy watching the effect of the water on the item they are painting?

## Tips

- ✿ Provide several buckets and plenty of painting materials so that everyone can participate.
- ✿ In winter, fill spray bottles with colored water and paint the snow.

---

**Sensory** 👂 👁

**30+ months**

**Outdoors**

**Prep Time** ⏱ **5 minutes**

**Benefits**
- ✿ Promotes visual and tactile stimulation
- ✿ Encourages understanding of cause and effect
- ✿ Develops fine motor skills

**Materials**
- ☑ Water
- ☑ Buckets
- ☑ Spray bottles
- ☑ Large paintbrushes with handles
- ☑ Sponges

# Making Pretzels

## What to do

1. Give each child a small piece of prepared dough to work with. Invite them to roll and shape it as they choose.
2. Grease a cookie sheet, and help the children place their pretzel shapes onto it, leaving at least two inches between pretzels.
3. In the small mixing bowl, combine the egg with one tablespoon water. Brush this mixture onto the pretzels, then sprinkle them with the coarse salt. If children are likely to touch the egg mixture, make this an adult-only step.
4. Bake for 20 minutes at 425°F, allow to cool, then eat and enjoy!

## What to look for

- How do the children react to the texture of the dough?
- How do they respond to the finished product?

## Tips

- Tape down pieces of waxed paper to reduce sticking, then pick up the waxed paper to move the pretzel to the baking sheet.
- Encourage the children to help with the cleanup. Give them wet sponges and invite them to scrub!

**Sensory** 👂 👁

**30+ months**

**Messy Area**

**Prep Time** 🕐 **20 minutes**

**Benefits**

- ✿ Promotes tactile and olfactory stimulation
- ✿ Develops understanding of cause and effect
- ✿ Encourages cooperation

**Materials**

- ☑ Pretzel dough (preferably made with children's help, see recipe on following page)
- ☑ Clean tabletop
- ☑ Small bowl
- ☑ Egg
- ☑ Fork
- ☑ Water
- ☑ Tablespoon
- ☑ Pastry brush
- ☑ Coarse salt
- ☑ Baking sheet

# Pretzel Recipe

## What to do

1. Wash hands.
2. Preheat oven to 425° F.
3. In the large mixing bowl, invite children to help you combine 1½ cups warm water with the yeast. Let it sit for five minutes, until it becomes bubbly. Encourage children to look for the bubbles. Talk to them about yeast and why we use it.
4. In the medium bowl, help children combine 3 cups of the flour with the sugar and table salt.
5. Add this dry mixture to the yeast, and mix it well. It should be very sticky.
6. Place the dough onto a lightly floured kneading surface, and slowly knead in another cup of flour. Encourage children to take turns kneading for five minutes after flour is combined, until the dough becomes smooth and no longer sticky.

## What to look for

* Are the children able to take turns and work together?
* Are they interested in the mixing process?

## Tips

* Have several different measuring utensils handy to reduce the time children have to wait before they can participate.
* Assign children tasks ahead of time, and remind them often of when it will be their turn. They will be able to be more patient if they are sure that they will have a turn soon.

**Sensory** 👂 👁

**Prep Time** ⏱ **10 minutes**

**Ingredients**
1½ cups warm water
1 teaspoon yeast
4+ cups flour
1 tablespoon sugar
1 teaspoon table salt
2 mixing bowls (large and medium)
1 mixing spoon
Measuring cups and spoons

# Index

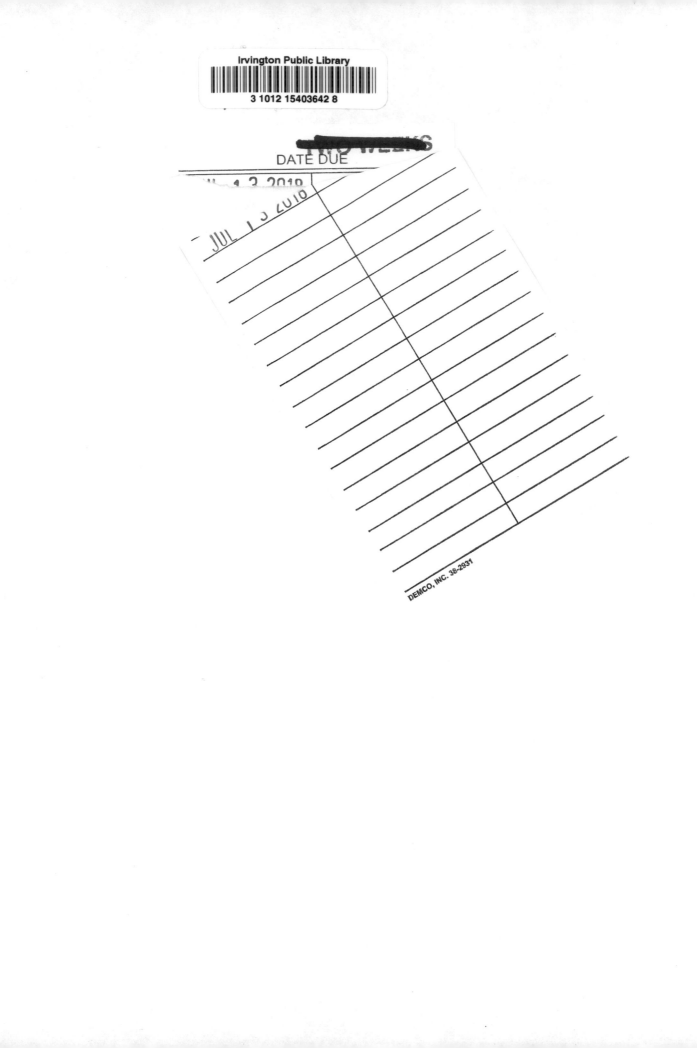

DATE DUE

JUL 1 3 2018

JUL 1 3 2018

DEMCO, INC. 38-2931